A GUIDE TO DEVELOPING THE ICT CURRICULUM FOR EARLY CHILDHOOD EDUCATION

A GUIDE TO DEVELOPING THE ICT CURRICULUM FOR EARLY CHILDHOOD EDUCATION

Iram and John Siraj-Blatchford

Trentham Books

Stoke on Trent, UK and Sterling, USA

Trentham Books Limited
Westview House   22883 Quicksilver Drive
734 London Road   Sterling
Oakhill   VA 20166-2012
Stoke on Trent   USA
Staffordshire
England ST4 5NP

First published 2006
Reprinted 2007

British Library Cataloguing-in-Publication Data
A catalogue record for this book is available from the British
Library

ISBN-13: 978-1-85856-300-8

Designed and typeset by Trentham Print Design Ltd, Chester
and printed in Great Britain by Cromwell Press Ltd, Trowbridge.

EARLY EDUCATION

The British Association for Early Childhood Education (Early
Education), founded in 1923, is the leading national voluntary
organisation for early years practitioners and parents with
members and branches in England, Northern Ireland, Scotland
and Wales.

Early Education promotes the right of all children to education of
the highest quality. It provides support, advice and information
on best practice for everyone concerned with the education and
care of young children from birth to eight.

Early Education, 136 Cavell Street, London E1 2JA
020 7539 5400
office@early-education.org.uk
www.early-education.org.uk

Contents

Dedication

To our Godchildren
Ben (3) and Emily (1)

Acknowledgements

This book would not have been possible without the cooperation and support of the primary schools, nursery schools, the headteachers, parents, children and staff we have worked with over the past six years.

In particular we want to thank *Ingrid Lemon, Rachel Ager, Angela Williams, Rita Wrightson, Sue Lane and Karen Dennison* and all of the Northamptonshire Lead Reception Teachers (LRTs) who worked so hard to make the **Northamptonshire ICT Strategy** a success. Most of the practitioners we cite (unless stated otherwise) are from Northamptonshire schools.

We would also like to thank the staff, parents and children at the **Gamesley Early Excellence Centre** for the privilege of working with them and for their permission to describe their achievements. Special thanks are due to *Lynn Kennington*, the head of Centre, and their two ICT coordinators *Carole Bennett* and *Cathy Jones* who made direct contributions to the text of Chapter 6. The Centre ICT policy is quoted in full at the end of that chapter. Further information, training and development resources are also available from the Centre website: http://www.gamesleyeec.org.uk

Thanks are due to our friends at **Early Education** (The British Association for Early Childhood Education – BAECE) for encouraging us to write the book, and for initially commissioning us to conduct the UK evaluation of KidSmart. We have been working closely with them and with the international EMEA team at **IBM** for several years now as the KidSmart project has progressed, so *Jenny Rabin* and *Liz Hodgkins* at Early Education, and *Marite Stragier, Carol Berry* and *Mark Wakefield* at IBM all deserve a special mention.

Vasiliki Repana supported our data collection for the initial UK KidSmart evaluation and *Ray Arnold* contributed significantly to the evaluations carried out for Kinderet and for the European KidSmart project. In the later study, we were also aided and abetted by *Hans Eirich* (Staatsinstitut fur Fruhpadagogik, Germany), *Maria-Jose Lera* (Spain), *Franca Rossi* and *Marcello Visocchi* (Universita La Sapienza, Italy), *Francis Strayer* (Universite de Toulouse, France) and *Maria Assunção Folque* and *Jose Luis Ramos* (Universidade de Évora, Portugal).

The 'Video Conferencing' study reported upon in Chapter 2 was completed on a very small budget and wouldn't have been possible without the support of *Dinara Petreyava* in collecting the data. We would also like to thank *Malva Villalon* for her support in triangulating our analysis.

Finally, we would finally like to thank our research collaborators in three EU funded projects:

Children's Awareness of Technology (CHAT)

Ingrid Pramling Samuelsson, Mikael Alexandersson and *Jonas Ryberg* (University of Goteborg, Sweden). *Anna-Lena Östern* and *Marina Lundkvist* (Åbo Akademi University, Finland)

Developmentally Appropriate Technology in Early Childhood (DATEC)

Ingrid Pramling Samuelsson (University of Goteborg, Sweden) and *Lena Magnusson* (Chalmers Tekniska Högskola). *Maria Assunção Folque* (Universidade de Évora, Portugal) and *Francisco Pacheco* (Associação de Profissionais de Educação do Norte Alentejo)

Educative Technologies in Kindergarten Context (Kinderet)

Vito José de Jesus Carioca, Sandra Saúde, Aldo Passarinho and *Bárbara Esparteiro* at Escola Superior de Educação de Beja, Portugal. *Ingrid Pramling Samuelsson* and *Sonja Sheridan* of Goteborg University, Sweden. *Rosa Nuez Martínez* and *María José Álvarez* of Fondo Promoción de Empleo, Asturias, Spain. *Lyubomir Genov* and *Korneia Genova* of Association 'RegioNet', Varna, Bulgaria.

Any shortcomings in this book are entirely those of the authors.

Preface

This is a book primarily for early childhood practitioners, managers and curriculum developers. While the book has been written to provide a practical guide to curriculum development, it is informed by our work on a number of major research initiatives. Curriculum guidance materials, developed as part of the EU funded *Developmentally Appropriate Technology in Early Childhood* (DATEC) project, were further elaborated in our evaluation of the IBM *KidSmart* initiative. Training analysis has been carried out in another EU supported project; *Kinderet*, and also in our work on curriculum development with Gamesley Early Excellence Centre and evaluating the *Northamptonshire's Foundation Stage ICT strategy*. These projects have all been drawn upon to provide exemplifications of good practice.

Information and Communications Technologies (ICT) is defined here in its broadest sense, as involving computers but also much more than desktop computers, as we attempt to show how ICT can contribute to children's learning and how it may be integrated into a play based curriculum. Key areas of learning are identified, such as communication and collaboration, creativity, socio-dramatic play and learning to learn (or metacognition). While the text provides an introduction to the ICT requirements in the Curriculum Guidance for the Foundation Stage (children 3-5), the international relevance and implications of such provisions are explicitly addressed. It also provides a critical account of the 'digital divide' and suggests practical strategies for all the individuals and institutions working towards the achievement of social justice.

The authors provide concrete guidance for the development of centre based practice. In addition to guidance on curriculum integration, they address areas of ergonomics (how children should sit at the computer, for how long and what risks are known from research) and the selection of appropriate educational software for very young children. Emphasis is given to the processes of policy development and the realisation of change and specific guidance is provided on the use of development plans and evaluation tools. Evaluations of practice and policy development at the centre level are provided from the Gamesley Early Excellence Centre; at the local authority level with the Northamptonshire ICT Strategy; and at an international level with the IBM KidSmart initiative. In each case we have attempted to map the development of practice with vignettes of good practice in staff development, children's learning and their use of ICT, and in working with parents and the home learning environment.

Iram and John Siraj-Blatchford
October 2005

1

An Emergent Technology Curriculum

> Our society is now defined as the 'Information Society', a society in which low-cost information and ICT are in general use, or as the 'Knowledge (-based) Society', to stress the fact that the most valuable asset is investment in intangible, human and social capital and that the key factors are knowledge and creativity. *European Commission* (2001)

As Selwyn (2002) has noted, computers and other ICTs have been introduced into schools and the early years for a variety of reasons, but one reason has been to begin preparing children for their future lives in the Knowledge Society. Information and Communications Technology (ICT) has both generated and sustained the transformations now taking place in Western societies as they give up their industrial economic ambitions of the past to become information and knowledge based societies. If we are to identify the most appropriate basis for educating our youngest children about ICT, we must therefore begin by saying a few words about the kind of future society our education system is preparing (or ill preparing) the children to inhabit.

Technological innovation is now extremely rapid. Today's latest idea is swiftly superseded by something new, or becomes irrelevant in our rapidly changing socio-cultural and economic contexts. As we struggle to come to terms with our new information societies, new forms of work and work organisation are already emerging. Knowledge-workers are increasingly required to control their own learning, and critically evaluate and manipulate information in the development of new knowledge products. In response to these changes, educational systems, which were until very recently wholly committed to the task of inducting students into traditional forms of knowledge, are increasingly being called upon to reduce curriculum content and prioritise the teaching of systems and big ideas over detail. While the top priority used to be for children to gain fluency in established subject knowledge, it is now increasingly recognised that they should be developing capability in accessing or retrieving information – that is, learning to learn. Instead of simply acquiring knowledge for its own sake, they should be learning more about how to do things with it. They should learn to generate *new* knowledge from established knowledge.

In the field of technology, more than any other, we should recognise that the forms of *technological literacy* demanded by an information society cannot be achieved by identifying and teaching children *all* the understandings, skills and capabilities that constitute a knowledge of technology as it presents itself to us today. Just as literacy in language learning is more than just learning to read so technological literacy is more than just being able to operate or understand today's technology. In the process of exploring and applying technology children may develop a '...*structure of facts, concepts, principles, procedures, and phenomena*' that will provide resources for the '*cognitive activities of knowing, understanding and reasoning*' (Greeno, 1991: 174). It is these more general and basic conditions of knowing, understanding and reasoning that constitute technological literacy.

What this means in practice is that we should not attempt to break ICT Education down in terms of the multitude of separate skills and competences that make it up. If we do this many will in any event soon be redundant. What we need to do is provide activities that encourage children to explore the technological affordances of a variety of ICT tools and to encourage them to apply them – playfully in the early years – for a range of different purposes.

To fully appreciate the past developments and the prospects for developing computers in the early years it is instructive to consider the developments in schools. IT (later defined as ICT) was first introduced into the National Curriculum for England and Wales as an element of a much more general Technology Curriculum. This was subsequently changed to give IT greater status as a separate subject (Higgins, 1995). But the central aims of the Technology curriculum were to teach technological literacy partly through the evaluation of technological products and processes, and to develop technological capability through engaging students in the practical activity of designing and making things. The really important thing to note here was that it wasn't the products that the children made that were so important in all of this, it was rather what they learned in the process of making them. This is as relevant to ICT education today as it was to IT in the early 1990s.

In this context multi-purpose (or generic) software can be seen to have a great deal more potential than dedicated application software. Consider how many more things you can do (or design and make) with a floor turtle like Swallow System's Pixie, or the graphics, word and number processing, and logo packages provided in 2Simple's Early Learning Toolkit or Tizzy's First Tools (Softease)? Each offers considerably more possibilities than products such as Edmark's Milly's Math House or Fisher Price's Playtime. Generic software – a category that includes Microsoft's Word, Paint, PowerPoint and Moviemaker – provides us with 'tools' that can be 'applied' for a variety of purposes.

In addition to these concerns to support children in developing technological literacy and in an effort to encourage greater integration of ICT across the curriculum, ICT educational policy in the UK has also stressed the importance of applying ICT to enhance learning in other areas of the curriculum. *The Early Learning Goals* in the *Curriculum Guidance for the Foundation Stage* (CGFS) (QCA, 2000) suggest that, by the end of the reception year, most children should be able to:

> Find out about, and identify the uses of technology in their everyday lives and use computers and programmed toys to support their learning. (QCA, *op cit*)

Some serious concerns have been raised about the sedentary nature of computer use and the potentially damaging effects of inappropriate ergonomics (Healey, 1998, Cordes and Miller, 2000). Plowman and Stephen (2003) provide a particularly critical account of the use of desktop computers (p11) and argue for the development of new technologies more appropriate for the early years (see also Siraj-Blatchford, 2004). The DATEC guidance (see below) suggests that the ergonomic difficulties associated with young children using desktop computers might be overcome by adopting applications that involve the children in working away from the computer part of the time (Siraj-Blatchford I. and J., 2000). As long as suitable seating, cushions and foot-rests are provided, children may be usefully taught to take some responsibility themselves for these aspects of health and safety from an early age.

Using ICT to support early learning

But current research into the use of ICT to promote learner achievement is not encouraging at any level of education. As David Wood (2003) has argued, the IMPACT-2 study commissioned by the Department for Education and Skills 'failed to provide any uniform evidence of links between school ICT and learner achievement' (p9). However, the use of ICT in schools at that time was still quite limited:

> Since time on task remains one of the best indicators of progress in learning, this finding implies that ICT uses have hardly been tested at or anywhere near the limit. Hence, *it is not clear whether current evidence represents a test of the educational potential of the technology or simply acts as an indicator of limitations of current practice in providing enough access for its use.* (p10, *op cit*, authors' emphasis)

Little in the way of systematic research and review has so far been carried out in the area of ICT in early childhood but what little evidence there is suggests a similar story.

A significant meta-analysis of the evidence related to the specific application of computers applied in support of beginning reading instruction was carried out by Blok *et al* (2002). This review looked at 42 studies published since 1990 comprising a total of 75 experimental comparisons involving early readers aged from 65 to150 months. On average, each child spent 35 minutes a week working with a wide range of applications developed as extensions to, or the replacement of, some element (or elements) of a regular reading programme. While the authors were cautious about their findings due to the poor quality of many of the individual studies, the overall effect size that they found was 0.2.[1] What may be even more significant is that effect sizes were found to be higher for those groups scoring more highly in pre-tests. Thus it was the more able students who did better with computer based instruction. While focused on a wider age group, other studies e.g. that conducted by the US National Reading Panel (National Institute of Child Health and Human Development, 2000) have shown more general positive effects.

So there does appear to be some limited evidence that computer based instruction may be effective in some areas of the early years curriculum. But the difficulty with this is that while a number of other longitudinal studies have shown us that children provided with predominantly direct or programmed instruction, without the use of a computer, sometimes do better academically in the short term than those provided with other forms of pedagogy (Marcon, 2002), we know that many of these gains are short lived. Highly structured, didactic teaching has also been found to result in young children showing significantly increased stress/anxiety behaviour (Burts *et al*, 1990). A longitudinal and rigorous study conducted by Schweinhart and Weikart (1997) for example showed little difference in the academic performance of young children provided exclusively with direct instruction, but they did find significantly more emotional impairment and disturbance leading to greater need for special educational provision.

Other studies have similarly shown that an exclusively didactic and formal approach to teaching young children can be counterproductive (Sylva and Nabuco, 1996). It has been found to hinder young children's learning, generate higher anxiety and lower self-esteem. While none of these studies were focused on computer based instruction, it seems extremely likely that the effects would be similar in the case of any programmed learning, particularly if they incorporated the kind of animation, sound or access level rewards and punishments found in many early years computer applications. It is for this reason that most authorities e.g. the Unites States, National Association for the Education of Young Children (NAEYC), Developmentally Appropriate Technology in Early Childhood (DATEC) consider the application of '*drill and practice*' software less appropriate in early childhood. Unfortunately this kind of software does continue to be applied. But as Clements (1994) put it a decade ago: 'What we as early childhood educators are presently doing most often with computers is what research and [NAEYC] guidelines say we should be doing least often' (p. 33).

As Clements (2002) argues in the context of maths instruction:

> ...drill and practice software can help young children develop competence in counting and sorting. However, it is questionable if the exclusive use of such software would subscribe to the vision of the National Council of Teachers of Mathematics to be 'mathematically literate' in a world where 'mathematics is rapidly growing and is extensively being applied in diverse fields.' Other types of programs, including computer manipulatives and other problem-solving programs, appear to hold more promise in this regard.

The conclusions to be drawn from this research are clear. If we are to use ICT to support early learning across the curriculum then the technology should be integrated to support the development of positive dispositions towards learning (see also Dweck, 2000, Carr and Claxton, 2002). The most appropriate curriculum model to draw upon is therefore arguably an *emergent* one.

Advocates of emergent literacy encourage mark making as a natural prelude to writing. They teach children the communicative value of the written word before they begin to focus on the technical skills (Hall, 1987). Similarly, advocates of an emergent approach to numeracy prioritise the early development of children's appreciation of the practical value of numbers (e.g. in counting). In the same way, we can encourage young children to apply ICT tools for their own purposes in their play as a natural prelude to formal ICT education in the school. If we adopt an *integrated emergent* approach, we will be providing opportunities for children to appreciate the use of written language and number at the same time.

Teachers who teach emergent literacy also read different kinds of text to children, and the emergent numeracy curriculum is supported when teachers demonstrate the value of basic skills for a wide range of purposes. In the same way, in emergent ICT we can introduce children to new hardware and software tools and applications, and we can draw upon their own experiences of adult interactions with ICT at supermarket checkouts, bank cash points etc. We can also involve the children in applying a range of computer applications to help us in our day to day work as teachers. In doing so, teachers are providing positive role models by showing children the value they place in their own use of literacy, numeracy and ICT.

Integration of ICT in Early Childhood

As the Early Learning Goals suggest, pre-school children should be finding out about and identifying the uses of technology in their everyday lives, and they should also be using computers and programmed toys to support their learning. The English curriculum guidance also usefully suggests that we should encourage children to observe and talk about the use of ICT in the environment on local walks, for example traffic lights, telephones, street lights, bar-code scanners of prices in shops.

> Using appropriately designed and supported computer applications, the ability to learn, move, communicate, and recreate are within the reach of all learners. Yet, with all these enhanced capabilities, this technology requires thoughtful integration into the early childhood curriculum, or it may fall far short of its promise. Educators must match the technology to each child's unique special needs, learning styles, and individual preferences.[2]

Evidence from studies in the UK show that there is enormous scope for the integration of technology into young children's play environments. Outdoor play vehicles, and other toys may be controlled by traffic lights; we can draw attention to the need for home corner washing machines to be programmed for different fabrics. We can encourage the use of pretend – or functioning – telephones, cash registers, office photocopiers, supermarket bar code scanners and computers, in socio-dramatic role play. Functioning computers can also be integrated into the children's pretend play, and successful trials have been conducted using suitable software and touch screens in play travel agent, office, and shop environments.

Image 1   Images 1 and 2 illustrate how teachers at Gamesley Early Excellence Centre followed up on a visit to a supermarket to look at the point of sale technology. The children had identified the barcodes used in the store and learned about the stock control and price information they carried. When they returned to the Centre a socio-dramatic play area was adapted for them to act out and explore this technological application further.

Improved awareness is likely to influence further progress as computers become more widely used by young children. But what is vital is the integration of technology across the entire curriculum, not opting for separate computer suites. As the UK evaluation of the IBM KidSmart pro-

Image 2   gramme found: 'Children need to see ICT used in a meaningful context and for real purposes,' (Siraj-Blatchford and Siraj-Blatchford, 2000). Image 3 shows a teacher supporting a child in using a KidSmart Early Explorer unit in a UK pre-school. Further details of the Kid-Smart initiative are provided in Chapter 8.

The notion of developing an emergent awareness and an ability to manipulate symbols is clearly recognised in the context of emergent literacy and numeracy, where educators specifically encourage the child to recognise the value of using words and numbers to represent artefacts and to quantify them, a form of managing information. But a great

deal can be done to promote these processes in the wider play context and in
children's play with technological toys.
Many settings use computer programmes
which manage information as part of
their project work. We have seen examples
of adults and children collecting information on a topic about the body and using
these data to make simple graphs e.g. of
eye colour or height.

Another important reason for employing
an integrated approach to ICT is the recognition that this is more consistent
with the notion of ICT products as tools. Tools are designed to be applied
for particular purposes when required; they are not usually designed for
continuous use for their own sake! The common practice of operating a
rota for children to gain access to computers may be seen as entirely
contrary to this approach. Equally inappropriate is the common practice
of providing access as a reward (or punishment).

Image 3

The European IBM KidSmart evaluation (Siraj-Blatchford and Siraj-
Blatchford, 2004) found that computers were being integrated more
closely into the curriculum in most countries, and that this was more
apparent in the area of socio-dramatic role play rather than in terms of
the equipment being used as a tool in wider learning processes – e.g. in
making greeting cards to be printed and then decorated, or using applications such as 'Build a Bug' in Millie's Math House, as a computer
assisted design (CAD) application to design Bugs that might then be constructed using playdough, plasticine or recycled materials.

Developmentally Appropriate Technology in Early Childhood (DATEC)

The kind of early and emergent ICT curriculum that education for a
Knowledge Society appears to demand was at first promoted by the
Developmentally Appropriate Technology in Early Childhood (DATEC)
project funded by the European Commission CONNECT programme in
2000/2001[3]. The DATEC partners worked with pre-schools in the UK,
Sweden and Portugal to identify examples of good practice that could be
tested and elaborated in each of the partner countries before being
accepted for publication as exemplars. Analysis of these exemplars led to

the development of guidance material for parents and early childhood educators. The DATEC research found that the best applications:

- *Were educational* – applications employed in the early years should be educational in nature and this effectively excludes all applications where clear learning aims cannot be identified. For example, it was found that, however entertaining, most arcade type games provided little encouragement of creativity, or indeed any other worthwhile learning outcome

- *Encouraged collaboration* – in the early years we know that activities that provide contexts for collaboration are especially important

- *Supported integration* – with an integrated approach to ICT we pre–sent ICT products as tools

- *Supported play* – play and imitation are primary contexts for representational and symbolic behaviour, and role-play is therefore central to the processes of learning in the early years

- *Left the child in control* – ICT should be controlled by the child, not control the child through programmed learning

- *Were transparent and intuitive* – applications should be selected that provide transparency: their functions should be clearly defined and intuitive

- *Avoided violence or stereotyping* – where applications fail to meet these criteria it would be difficult to justify their use in any educational context

- *Supported the development of an awareness of health and safety issues* – where the use of a computer is integrated with other activities e.g. in socio-dramatic play, modelling, painting etc. children benefit from greater movement and exercise away from the computer

- *Supported the involvement of parents* – studies have shown that when parents, teachers and children collaborate towards the same goals it leads to improved academic performance

This emergent and integrated ICT curriculum model has been elaborated further in Siraj-Blatchford and Whitebread (2003), Siraj-Blatchford and Siraj-Blatchford (2004) and in this book. In these later works, the quality of exemplary ICT applications has been increasingly seen in terms of their potential for supporting the development of *com-*

munication and collaboration, children *learning to learn* (meta-cognition), and creativity. We are at an early stage in the development of curriculum objectives of this kind, but as Loveless (2002) has noted, these imperatives are increasingly being recognised throughout education: Each of these themes will be introduced below and then elaborated upon further in Chapters 2 and 3.

The application of ICTs to support communication and collaboration

There is general agreement among developmental psychologists and educationalists that collaboration is especially important in the early years. It is also within communicative and collaborative contexts that creativity and metacognition are developed in early childhood. When children share joint attention, or engage jointly in activities we know that this provides a significant cognitive challenge in itself (Light and Butterworth,1992). Collaboration is also considered important in providing opportunities for cognitive conflict as efforts are made to reach consensus (Doise and Mugny, 1984), and for the co-construction of potential solutions in the creative processes. But, as Crook (2003) has argued, designers have too often assumed that their task has been to develop software that supports the learner in solitary acts of learning.

What they have failed to recognise is the fact that the private reflection and interrogation required to learn on one's own are first developed through socially-organised learning (*op cit*). Also, while the value of ICT in supporting collaborative learning in schools has been demonstrated (Crook, 1994), successful collaboration does not automatically occur simply by bringing children together to share the same computer. As Crook (1994) has shown, teachers often need to orchestrate collaborative interactions if there are to be learning gains. He warns us that:

> ...while there is considerable evidence that ICT can be a powerful resource in helping to support joint working and classroom collaboration between school age pupils, it must be recognised that the social systems of pre-school environments have different dynamics. (Crook, 2003, p13)

Programmable toys and many, if not most, screen based applications do offer the possibility of collaboration in terms of symbolic manipulation, but adult intervention is often needed to gain the most from software even when it has been designed to facilitate collaborative problem solving, drawing, or construction. The UK Effective Provision of Pre-school Education (EPPE) project (Sylva *et al*, 2004), and the Researching Effective Pedagogy in the Early Years (REPEY) report (Siraj-Blatchford *et al*, 2002) studies have found that the most effective foundation stage settings combined the provision of free play opportunities with more focused group work involving adult direct instruction. This more balanced approach would therefore appear to be the most desirable model to promote with ICT as well.

As we see in Chapter 2, the EPPE/REPEY research also suggests that adult-child interactions that involved some element of sustained shared thinking are especially valuable in terms of children's early learning. These were identified as sustained verbal interactions that moved forward in keeping with the child's interest and attention. These were initiations that were most commonly elicited in practical activity and they may often occur in the context of children's use of ICT. Unfortunately, as we shall see, the evidence suggests that too often there will be no adult present at these times to provide the necessary scaffolding and support.

The application of ICTs to support learning to learn (metacognition)

Plowman and Stephen (2003) cite Haugland (2000) and Yelland (1999) in arguing that many practitioners have felt that screen-based activities are less effective than three-dimensional manipulatives. But others have argued that computers provide a means by which young children may be supported in their manipulation of symbols and representations on the screen in a useful manner that allows them to distance themselves from the signifying objects. Screen-based activities might therefore support the processes of verbal reflection and abstraction (Forman, 1984). This theme is specifically addressed by Bowman *et al* (2001) in the US National Research Council's report *Eager to Learn: Educating our Preschoolers*. The report strongly endorses the application of computers in early childhood:

> Computers help even young children think about thinking, as early proponents suggested (Papert, 1980). In one study, pre-schoolers who used computers scored higher on measures of metacognition (Fletcher-Flinn and Suddendorf, 1996). They were more able to keep in mind a number of different mental states simultaneously and had more sophisticated theories of mind than those who did not use computers. (p229)

The Concise Dictionary of Psychology defines metacognition as: having knowledge or awareness of one's own cognitive processes (Statt, 1998). Metacognition has been associated with effective learning in numerous contexts (Larkin, 2000), and the concept has been applied by educators seeking to design effective pedagogy. There is a general consensus that metacognition develops as the individual finds it necessary to describe, explain and justify their thinking about different aspects of the world to others (Perner *et al*, 1994; Pelligrini, Galda, and Flor, 1997; Lewis *et al* , 1996). For most children such a theory of mind develops at about 41/2 years (Tan-Niam *et al*, 1999). Research shows that children's pretend play becomes reciprocal and complementary at about the same time (Howes and Matheson, 1992). Research has established that a child with a theory of mind is able to understand that other people have minds of their own, that other individuals have their own understandings and motivations, and that they usually act according to their own understanding and motivations, even when they are mistaken.

All this idicates that the applications likely to be effective in supporting the development of metacognition are those also that are most effective in supporting socio-dramatic play. These are also the applications that tend to be more effective in supporting communication and collabora-tion.

The application of ICTs to support creativity

A good way to understand the development of young children's creativity may be to consider it in terms of the development and manipulation of schemes (Siraj-Blatchford, J. 2004). For Piaget (1969) and other develop-mental psychologists, a scheme is an operational thought: it may be a recalled behaviour, the recollection of a single action or a sequence of actions. To be creative, children need to acquire a repertoire of schemes, and they also need the playful disposition to try out these schemes in new contexts. These trials may be expressed verbally, in the mind's eye, or in the material world. Young children are naturally curious and they learn many of their schemes vicariously; they spontaneously imitate a wide range of the schemes provided by adults and other children. Vygotsky (2004) distinguished between two types of activity, the '*repro-ductive*', and those involving 'combinations' or creativity: '*Creative activity, based on the ability of our brain to combine elements, is called imagination or fantasy in psychology*' (p4). In their fantasy play, young children quite naturally separate objects and actions from their meaning in the real world and give them new meanings. They should be en-couraged to communicate these creative representations because it is in this way that their powers of expression and abstraction may be developed more generally (Van Oers, 1999).

12

Educators may encourage the discovery of schemes and provide explicit models for the children to follow in their play. This can be regularly supported by innovative early years practitioners using ICT. Both real and pretend ICTs may be integrated in support of socio-dramatic play and this kind of play is widely recognised to be of significant cognitive and socio-emotional benefit (Smilansky, 1990, p35). Computer applications such as SEMERC's 'At the Café' and 'At the Vet's' allow children to imitate adult role behaviours, acting them out in their play and learning to understand them better. Pretend telephones, domestic equipment and point of sale technologies are employed to support children in their imitations and simulations of the adult world and human relationships through symbolic representation. Practitioners are also able to create supportive resources of their own using generic office tools such as word-processors, paint and PowerPoint applications, and ICT has also been found to support creative socio-dramatic activity quite spontaneously. For example, Brooker and Siraj-Blatchford (2002) found that children often make little distinction between the on-screen and the off-screen world:

> On-screen images were 'grabbed', scolded, fingered and smacked, with dramatic effect, as part of the small-group interaction with the software. In some instances, they took on an off-screen life of their own, as children continued the game the computer had initiated, away from the machine. (*op cit*, p267)

Well-designed on-screen applications provide for a wide variety of possible responses by the children. Adventure games and simulations often offer particular strengths. They also allow the child to try things out and, if they don't work, to try something else.

Socio-dramatic play

The Early Years practitioners we have worked with have shown that there is enormous scope for the integration of ICT into young children's pretend play environments. Outdoor play vehicles and other toys may be controlled by traffic lights; home corner washing machines may be programmed for different fabrics; children are already using pretend (and sometimes functioning) telephones, cash registers, office photocopiers, supermarket bar code scanners, desk top computers, etc. in their socio-dramatic role play. Functioning computers can also be integrated into the children's pretend play and successful experiments have been conducted using suitable software and touch screens in simulated travel agents, offices, and shop environments. The possibilities are endless and the learning potential considerable. While there is clearly a need for more in the way of ICT props – both software and hardware – to be developed, a great deal can be achieved by innovative practitioners working with the children in creating their own improvisations.

In one Northamptonshire reception classroom, for example, we found that Brilliant Computing's 'At the Vet's' programme encouraged emergent writing (Image 4):

Image 4

> The children have all been desperate to have a go at this one and demonstrating it on the whiteboard was a very effective way of showing the children how to use the programme...this programme has seen some excellent cooperative play, with children helping each other to type in their names, pointing out the correct letters on the keyboard. As well as supporting the children's letter recognition and early attempts at spelling, some children have been more confident in themselves as emergent writers saying 'I can do anything I like' whilst tying in letter strings. The children have loved printing out the bills and have used these to present to the 'vet' as a treatment regime. (Chrissie Dale, King's Sutton School)

This application was developed to incorporate a Listening Station as a telephone answering machine (Image 5). And the activity considered promising enough to commit further time and effort to develop it further:

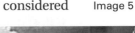

Image 5

> Some of the children have started pretending to write the messages down but I have not yet observed them taking these messages into their play. I need to rerecord the messages as the volume levels are uneven and they need more careful thinking out to vary the play they might develop. I need to buy a tape with the shortest running time I can find or might even buy a cheap answering machine or ask parents to donate an old one. (*op cit*)

In another classroom an elaborate drama was developed (Image 6):

> When we first set up the role-play area, we visited the local Post Office to look at, and photograph, the items and technology that we would need in our School Post Office. Back at school, I displayed the photographs on the classboard [interactive whiteboard] and we talked about how they worked and their importance in the Post Office. In small groups the children built their own computer and security system... At the beginning of the week, I knew the Learning Objectives upon which I was going to focus. However, the children became so involved in the experience that many more were eventually covered at the end of the week than originally planned. Throughout the week, the children worked together through 'sustained shared thinking' ...to solve the crime. By the end of the week, the children were listening to each other's ideas without the level of adult intervention that was needed at the beginning of the week. (Kathryn Syree, Syresham School)

> I set up a burglary in the Post Office, imagining that the robber had been caught on video by the children's security camera and video system. Before this week's work I had filmed a member of staff dressed in black

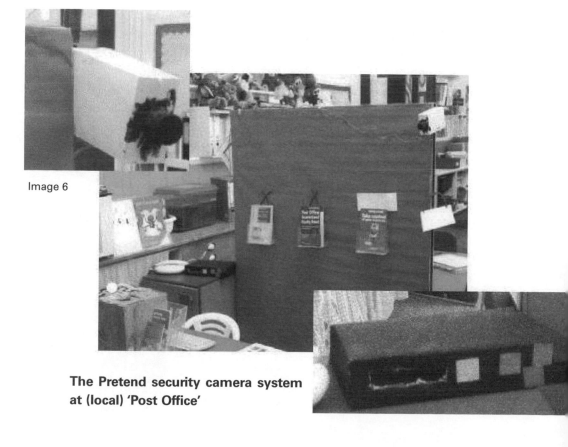

Image 6

The Pretend security camera system at (local) 'Post Office'

with pink flower on her hat robbing the Post Office, so the children had to find this video tape. The children rotated around different activities to help solve the crime. They used the digital camera to photograph evidence, the classboard and Easiteach [whiteboard software] to make leaflets to hand out around school, the tape player to record the Police interviews. On Friday the children had found the tape and sat transfixed as they watched the burglary take place. On the first play of the tape the children could not quite believe what they were seeing! ...All the children took part in and enjoyed the week's activities because they all wanted to achieve the end goal of catching the burglar. This enthusiasm spread around the school, with many children discussing who could have burgled the Reception Class Post Office. Word even spread to the local Post Office in the village. The discussions between children, parents and villagers demonstrated the power and effect that this combination of ICT and role-play had had on the children's learning... (Kathryn Syree, Syresham School)

In another Northamptonshire classroom, Helen Morrall and Antonia Curson drew on extracts of the movie Apollo 13, NASA web resources, and a range of ICTs to develop a project on Space travel. A play area was developed as 'mission control' and the children communicated between that and the 'launch pad' with walkie talkies. A PC tablet PowerPoint presentation provided all of the count down safety checks in preparation for blast off (a clipart animation) (Image 7).

Images 7 and 8

The children were immediately motivated by the context and developed some simple story ideas when they started to play in the space rocket. The keyboard, 'monitor', buttons and dials in the space rocket were used appropriately and often engaged pairs of children in dialogue about what they were doing. For example, H (pressing keys on the keyboard): 'ssssssshhhh look there's fire' to E. who responds 'all the people are getting out of the way'. This discussion of the rocket launch demonstrated the effectiveness of the video images they had seen to develop their imaginative play. Similarly the play tools were regularly used for 'fix' the rocket and the children often discussed what they tools did. (Helen Morrall, St Barnabas School)

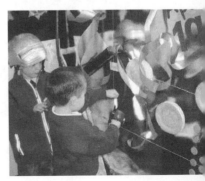

The drama was structured at various points as messages from Mission Control were delivered to stimulate further play. The project encouraged a good deal of sustained shared thinking. It also encouraged collaborative play (Image 8):

> ...One child put on his astronaut suit and pretended to walk around in space, slowly bobbing up and down with arms outstretched to imitate the moon walk. I noted how the keyboard was in almost constant use, the children taking turns to sit on the chairs and use the 'computer'. Some children sat together pressing the buttons and looking at the 'screen' and I felt that this ICT resource was successfully encouraging some collaborative play. (Antonia Curson, St Barnabas School)

> ... Many children were keen to use the tablet but needed time to familiarise themselves with it first. It also took some adult intervention for them to incorporate it into their play. For example, one child sat with the tablet for a long time, very engrossed in the programme but showing no signs of collaboration with others. I gave him suitable time to explore the tablet independently, working out how to use the pen effectively and looking at all the different screens. I then suggested that he should let the astronauts in the rocket know that he was getting ready for 'blast off', encouraging him to involve the other children in his 'rocket checks'. He responded well to these ideas, by now having the confidence to use the tablet in his play. He even used the telephones alongside the tablet to let the astronauts know that his 'checks' were finished. The tablet also encouraged some good shared thinking about how to use it, with use of some appropriate technical language. For example, I watched as two boys came over to explore it. 'Shall I help you?'...'You have to press the arrow'... 'Let's do that one now'... 'Press it, press it'. (Antonia Curson, St Barnabas School)

Notes

1 As Blok *et al* suggest, an effect size of 0.2 is usually considered to be small but we do need to put this in context. As Coe (2002) has argued, for a school in which 50% of pupils were previously gaining five or more A* – C grades, an effect size of 0.2 would raise this percentage to 58%. So, although research convention suggests that a 0.2 effect size is small, an improvement on this scale might actually be considered quite substantial by most practitioners and policy makers.

2 NAEYC National Association for the Education of Young Children Position Statement Technology and Young Children: Ages 3 through 8 (Adopted April 1996)

3 See http://www.ioe.ac.uk/cdl/DATEC

2

Using Technology for Communication and Collaboration

Supporting communication and collaboration

Chapter 1 focuses mainly on the use of desktop computers in the pre-school as is appropriate, in light of the rather short time that computer applications have been available for use in early childhood. But in the adult world, desktop computers have been around for decades, and various forms of laptop and handheld computers are already taking their place. Furthermore, if we consider the use of computers more generally and the kind of applications of computers young children should be learning about, there is a vast range of technological systems and artefacts. An earlier text, written especially for parents and early educators, stressed the importance of developing readers' awareness of the diversity of the computer technology being applied around them (Siraj-Blatchford and Whitebread, 2003). It has sometimes been difficult to recognise all the computers around us, as they are increasingly embedded within other technological products. ICT has become an invisible yet ubiquitous force profoundly affecting our lives.

As well as traffic lights, bank cash points and shop checkouts, there are many everyday technologies that we take for granted. We may not know that mobile telephones incorporate microprocessors to control all the background communications that need to be made with their base stations in order to make and keep a connection throughout the call. Microprocessors are also used to perform high-speed signal-manipulation calculations and co-ordinate the operations of the customisable features on the phone such as the directory of numbers. Cars and other road vehicles are now routinely equipped with microprocessors to control the mixture of fuel and air entering the engine. Microprocessors may also be employed to control the antilock brakes, to operate the cruise control facility, and/or to provide information on fuel consumption. When a sales assistant swipes our credit card through the device or till, or we feed it into a slot on the till or at a bank cash point, we may realise that data recorded on the magnetic strip of the card is being read and transmitted directly to a local bank by a computer. But how often do we think about what happens next? The bank computer communicates the data electronically through the credit card network and passes back an authorisation for the transaction. At the same time the debit is recorded against our bank account, to be communicated back to us later in our monthly statement and bill.

> In fact a wide range of other products incorporate computers that are dedicated to particular functions, and these microcontrollers are included in modern cameras, camcorders, answering machines, laser printers, telephones (those with caller ID, number memories, etc.), as well as any refrigerators, dishwashers, ovens, washers or dryers that have displays and keypads. This is to say nothing about the multitude of uses in industry, in commerce and in the leisure industry. We are also certain to see more and more of these devices incorporated in the technology around us as new applications are found for them. (Siraj-Blatchford and Whitebread, 2003, p4).

So how do children learn about these technologies? What new opportunities for learning might they provide?

Social interaction in early childhood

Research suggests that early learning is an interactive event, in which children actively construct their own understandings within a social and physical environment. Much of the children's earliest learning is the product of interactions with adults and peers, even where there has been no deliberate attempt to instruct. Children learn a great deal from observing people more competent than themselves. We can draw upon the social cognitive theory of Bandura (1986) to account for the way in which the experience of social interaction (and media) provide for this kind of observational learning. For Bandura the process of social learning begins with 'imitative' learning which is subsequently internalised through identification and incorporated into the individual's self-concept. It is for this reason that the importance of early years educators modeling appropriate language, behaviours, skills and attitudes is especially recognised. Such modeling is likely to be consequential in terms of cognitive, social and dispositional outcomes.

Piaget described a learning mechanism which involved children in the active elaboration of their own mental structures as they assimilated and accommodated new experiences. But even when an experience contrasts markedly with some aspect of a child's prior learning, we can't take it for granted that children will learn from that experience. As Piaget argued in his early accounts of this learning process, learning may be triggered by the recognition of some 'disequilibrium' between the child's new phenomenon or experience and their prior knowledge and skill, but it is 'fuelled' by the *affect* of their 'interest'. For learning to take place, children need to be motivated to engage with the cognitive challenge presented. In the case of imitative learning children are often motivated by desire to 'be like' and/or 'to be liked' by the person imitated. In other cases we may need to make specific provision for their affective involvement. Interest in the new phenomenon or experience might arouse their spontaneous natural curiosity, but it could also be influenced by the adults and peers around them. Piaget argued that children's intellectual adaptation was therefore as much an adaptation to the social environment as it was an adaptation to their physical and material environment. This provides a potentially strong foundation for early years educational practice, as it accounts simultaneously for learning and for motivation.

Unfortunately, this latter part of Piaget's theory, which takes account of the role of social factors in early childhood development, has been largely neglected (DeVries, 1997). Yet Piaget argued that adult-child and peer relations influence every aspect of development and that affective and personality development are intimately related to intellectual and moral development. Perhaps most importantly, Piaget argued that reciprocity in peer relations provide the foundations for perspective taking and for decentring. This suggests that collaborative play is immensely important for children. According to DeVries, Piaget proposed ways in which co-operative social interaction between children and between children and adults function to promote cognitive, affective and moral development. As she says:

> If Piaget was correct, then we need to reconsider the structure and methods of our schools from the point of view of long-term effects on children's sociomoral, affective and intellectual development. (*ibid.*, p.16).

Two closely associated and large scale studies in the UK, the Effective Provision of Pre-school Education (EPPE) project, and the Researching Effective Pedagogy in the Early Years (REPEY) project, have also found that '*Sustained Shared Thinking*' (SST) episodes, where adults work with children to solve problems, clarify concepts, evaluate activities, or extend narratives etc., are strongly associated with effective educational practice in early childhood (Siraj-Blatchford *et al.*, 2002, p8). The model of inter-action identified in these early childhood studies may be considered comparable to Schaffer's (1996) 'joint involvement episodes' and the work carried out by Wells and Meija-Arauz (2001), who suggest that:

> ...there is increasing agreement among those who study classrooms that learning is likely to be most effective when students are actively involved in the co-construction of meaning through discussion of topics that are of significance to them.

Socio-dramatic play, with or without the use of ICT, provides contexts for children to share representations and to articulate their thinking, bringing to consciousness ideas that they are still only beginning to grasp intuitively (Hoyles, 1985). Some of the associated learning will involve learning about technology, but ICT may also be incorporated in the play. In time, the most significant ICTs in this respect may be those incorporated in children's toys. But little research has so far been carried out to study how 'intelligent toys' might be best employed. The work carried out by Luckin *et al* (2003), and in the i3 *Experimental School Environment* projects (Siraj-Blatchford, 2004) is, however, significant.

The CACHET (Computers And Children's Electronic Toys) project (Luckin *et al*, 2003, Plowman and Luckin 2003) studied young children's use of interactive toys such as Microsoft ActiMates *Barney*, *Arthur* and *D.W.* The toys have embedded sensors that could be squeezed to speak or, when (wirelessly) connected to a desktop computer, offers hints and tips to children as they play with the associated software. The researchers studied their responses and found that the children's interest in the toy waned quickly, with younger siblings expressing more interest. The pro-gramming of this first generation of 'smart' toys was found to be in-adequate for the age group. The researchers did find that the toys en-couraged a great deal more interactions between peers and over three times as many interactions with the researcher, suggesting that tangible, as opposed to screen-based, interfaces may have significant potential in future. It also seemed that the use of such toys might be instrumental in redressing the current gender imbalance in school use of computers.

The main objective of the *Children in Chros and Chronos* (C3) project (Ioannidou and Dimitracopoulou, 2004) was to develop game-like collaborative activities that promoted children's spatial-temporal awareness and cognition while developing specific skills like map reading. Global Positioning System (GPS) technology was applied in creating activities that demanded sophisticated communication between two groups of children. One group was located at a base workstation that ran the activity software and the other team moved around the activity environment carrying a high precision (+/- 1m) GPS device and communicating with the base team via walkie-talkies. The technology provided a way for the base-team to observe – in real time – the exact path taken by the mobile team. While completing their maps the children were able to use the walki-talkies to discuss what the important landmarks were and what icons might be used to represent them.

The i3 *KidStory project* (Stanton *et al*, 2004) team aimed to develop collaborative storytelling technologies. They initially extended the University of Maryland *KidPad* software, which provided a means by which a variety of tools could be employed to create/draw story objects and link these elements together to create narratives. When the children zoom in on a particular story object to work on, the *KidStory* extensions have allowed them to work in pairs operating multiple mice and other tools on the same screen. The project also involved the integration of a number of technologies into a 'magic carpet' which included arrays of pressure mats and physical props associated with either barcode or video tracking technologies that allowed them to navigate their stories.

The main aim of the i3 Nimis project (Cooper and Brna, 2004) was to develop a classroom of the future, using large touch sensitive display screens and smaller pen/stylus input Wacom workstations. The technology helped teachers provide more opportunities for collaboration through structured shared tasks, and supported spontaneous interactions involving pair work, group work, and whole class collaboration. The children were thus given more opportunities to collaborate and take on leadership roles that build their confidence and self-esteem. The use of speech synthesis was particularly successful.

One of the most intriguing findings of the i3 *Playground* project (Hoyles and Noss, 2004), which involved children developing their own 'virtual playgrounds', was how the online collaboration facilitated by the children sharing their games with 'critical friends' on the internet supported them in the process of developing or expressing system/formal rules as opposed to narrative accounts. It seems that in the absence of face-to-face communication and collaboration the children found it necessary to formalise their thinking. Similar processes may well have been involved when young children were engaged in range of applications involving online collaborative drawing using Microsoft's NetMeeting Video conferencing tools. This was a Portuguese ('Aproximar') initiative identified in the DATEC project in 1999[1]. The nursery schools involved were quite small and very isolated, as they are located in villages in the North of Alentejo. The internet was applied in a number of creative ways in order to support communication between both the children and the staff, and with the wider world. The communication network that they generated promoted social contacts, access to information and the exchange of information as well as collaborative learning in several curriculum areas (http://www.apena.rcts.pt/aproximar/). One of their applications involved groups of children aged 3 to 6 years from two nurseries writing a story together. The story was started by one group and sent to the other group through e-mail. After going back and forwards several times the story was finished and ready to be illustrated. Then each part of the story was illustrated collaboratively using the NetMeeting interface.

Numerous claims have been made about the potential of technology to change the traditionally accepted developmental limits on children's learning. Claims have also been made in the UK regarding the successful application of video conferencing in pre-schools. The DATEC initiative provided an ideal opportunity to conduct some formal trials. Studies of video conferencing initially using closed circuit television systems were conducted in two primary school reception classes and a local authority nursery in the UK. The 'conferencing' was initially conducted over short distances (5-10 metres) and was offered as a free choice play environment/activity.

Investigating the use of closed circuit television (CCTV)

A study by Tan-Niam *et al* (1999) had recently been published which directly addressed the question of how early childhood development influenced, and was influenced by, the initiation and reciprocity of children's play. Their methodology, which applied established tests of theory of mind (ToM), was adapted for our purposes. Children usually develop a ToM (the ability to recognise the independent thinking of other people) between 4 and 5 years of age. Tan-Niam *et al*'s (1998) previous work had already shown that children playing together who had a ToM interacted more than non-ToM children and that even when only one of the children involved had achieved ToM the children's social interaction was enriched. Tan-Niam *et al*'s (1999) study involved a video analysis of a sample of 48 groups of two children with a mean age of 52.5 months. For each pair, 20 minutes of pretend play was carried out in a 'semi-naturalistic' setting and then analysed and compared across the following dyad types:

1. ToM paired with non-Tom (TX)
2. ToM paired with ToM (TT)
3. Non-ToM paired with non- ToM (XX)

The analysis was carried out to identify both the initiation of play (play bids) and the level of reciprocity. Their findings suggested that:

- the ToM partners initiated more play bids (independent of age and gender)
- the XX dyads initiated less play bids that TT and TX dyads
- the TT dyads bid significantly more than TX dyads

These findings appear to support the findings of a number of family studies (including Dunn *et al*, 1991; Lewis *et al*, 1996) that the presence of a ToM child in an asymmetrical dyad might provide support within a 'zone of proximal development' (Vygotsky, 1978). A subsequent analysis (Tan-Niam *et al*, 2000) was conducted to further investigate the quality of the play involved. Two mutually exclusive coding categories were applied: visual regard and engagement of play. In this study, Tan-Niam *et al* provide the following operational definitions:

Table 1

Variable	Code	Operational Definitions
Visual Regard		
Divided	V1	Visual attention is divided or different
Scan	V2	Both partners scanning the environment or looking at camera/experimenter (visual regard in this case is off task)
Mutual prop/s	V3	Mutual visual attention on same props
Eye contact	V4	Making eye contact with partner
Play Engagement		
Non-interactive	S0	Not involved with specific person, object or activity
Other object	S1	Each child engaged with different objects and playing alone
Person directed	S2	Engaged in person play/verbal play only
Co-ordinated	S3	Co-ordinated partner-object play

Tan-Niam (2000) found that:

- the quality of the play by XX dyads was poor in terms of social interaction, as they tended to focus visually on different things and engage with different props.

- the play of TX dyads was significantly more interactive in terms of visual regard and play engagement than XX dyads and is similar to that of the TT dyads.

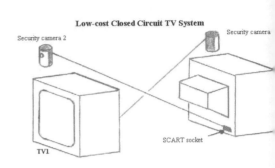

Image 9

While Tan-Niam *et al* provided props to encourage play according to a set theme (bathing and dressing a doll), we were anxious to provide a more 'natural' play environment in our study, where there was no pre-specification of the play context or any artificial pairing of the dyads. We were interested to see: (a) how the children spontaneously played with the CCTV apparatus, and (b) how their ToM influenced this spontaneous play (if at all).

The study was carried out in a reception classroom and involved 29 children (16 girls and 13 boys) with a mean age of 591/2 months. The apparatus involved the use of two inexpensive security cameras from a Do-it-Yourself superstore, attached to two television receivers using the regular SMART connection (see Image 9). The equipment was set up in an area immediately adjacent to the children's regular socio-dramatic 'home corner' play environment. No introduction or explanation was provided except to say that the equipment was for them to play with. In our first trial we collected a total of 117 minutes of uninterrupted video during three free play periods from a static camera set up to view both monitors. The researcher who was present during these recordings was familiar to the children, and by the time the data was collected they were used to there being a video camera in the room.

Figure 1

The children's play was analysed according to their 'visual regard' and play engagement, applying Tan-Niam's (2000) coding definitions. The analysis was blind since it was only after completing these observations that all the children's ToM capabilities were

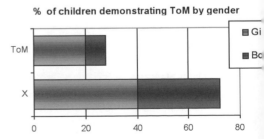

% of children demonstrating ToM by gender

assessed. For this purpose the standard 'unexpected transfer' (Wimmer and Perner, 1983) task designed to identify the child's ability in ascribing false beliefs was applied and the test was also adapted and extended to be carried out as a game using the CCTV apparatus. In the standard task, the child is told a false belief story e.g. that a child has hidden an object in one place and it is then moved without their knowledge. The child being assessed is asked whether the child who hid the object knows where it is and whether they remember the story, as both conditions must be met to ascribe ToM. In our study we prepared two boxes of identical objects (e.g. two paintbrushes, two flowerpots, two balls etc.) which differed in only one respect (e.g. size). Two adults were involved, one sitting with the child and the other at the other camera. The child was shown that the boxes held the same objects and was invited to take one box to the adult at the other camera so they could play a game together. Adult and child then chose a number of objects from their box without showing them and asked the adult on the screen to show them the one they had in their box. By prior arrangement, the object presented on screen failed in each case to match the one the child had selected, for instance a large paintbrush instead of a small one.

Only 28 per cent of the children in our opportunity sample demonstrated ToM in both tests, and age was clearly not a factor although gender may well have been. The size of our sample doesn't support any convincing statistical analysis of the issue but it may be significant that more than twice as many of the girls demonstrated ToM (Figure 1). In addition to the ToM tasks, we also asked each child at the start of the activity if the other adult – on the screen – could see them, and all said yes. They were then asked if there was any way that the child could stop the other adult seeing them. Most of the children responded to this by covering the screen or hiding. Only one child covered his face, and another suggested covering the eyes of the other adult. It may have been significant that none of the children covered the camera. We also asked the children if it would be possible to see themselves on the screen and only 47 per cent of the non-ToM children said no, whereas 71 per cent of the ToM children were adamant that it wasn't possible. As a follow-up prompt we asked them whether, if they ran around to the other screen, it would be possible to see themselves. Only one child managed to resist the temptation to do so...

The video data were coded every minute for visual regard and play engagement and this analysis was triangulated by an independent coder who was unaware of the children's ToM capabilities. Codes were only applied where both coders agreed. It was immediately clear from the analysis that the children's use of the technology was such that V4 and S3 codes were in almost 100 per cent correspondence. The technology clearly encouraged social interaction so that V4/S3 codes were applied for a full 62.4 per cent of the total time recorded and in all groups. In Tan-Niam's (2000) study the maximum frequency (of TT dyads) of eye contact recorded was 15.3 per cent, and in co-ordinated play 48.3 per cent (also TT dyads). The children usually played with the apparatus in groups of two or three, but at times groups of four or five were engaged in play with it. The children frequently alternated in making direct and then CCTV eye contact as a way of checking images with reality. In the early stages especially, there was a great deal of screen touching and tapping when they saw their peers on screen. Despite the small number of children who demonstrated ToM in the tasks, they were involved in 36.8 per cent of all the code V4/S3 behaviours. Thirteen point seven per cent of the coding related to groups including TT dyads and 23.1 per cent to groups that included one child demonstrating ToM. And 25.6 per cent of the V4/S3 codes were applied to non-ToM groups.

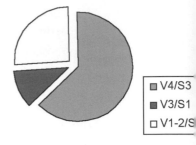

Frequency of codes as % of total time

V4/S3
V3/S1
V1-2/S

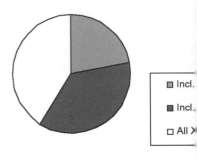

V4/S3 coding according to ToM

Incl.
Incl.
All X

Figures 2 and 3

There were also occasions when non-ToM individuals, pairs or groups of three children set up toys or other objects at one screen to view at the other, and these instances were coded as V3/S1. In only five cases the children played a game that involved hiding from each other, mostly by crawling under the table the monitor was sitting upon. The children who played this game all demonstrated ToM. The boys made greater use of the technology and were responsible for 53 per cent of the V4/S3 coding. However, if the contribution of just one boy to this, who was particularly fascinated and played frequently with both boys and girls, the girls' share of the coding increases to 56 per cent, which almost exactly matches their proportion of the overall sample.

Figure 4

V4/S3 sustained over 3 minutes

Incl.
Incl.
All X

The children who demonstrated ToM dominated the more sustained play with the CCTV, with five times as many T or TT groups as all the X-groups sustaining their play over three minutes. That said, the most sustained play of all, totalling 11 minutes, involved a group of three non-ToM children who discovered that the screen image could be inverted by turning the camera on the other monitor. As far as could be established the children seemed to view this operation in much the same way as they might the use of a joy stick or other remote control device. In these early stages of exploration there was no evidence of the children recognising the function of the security cameras for themselves. No lens was visible, and it is likely that they weren't recognised by any of the children as cameras at all, although individuals *did* speculate at times about the possible involvement of our static research camera in what was going on.

Throughout the study the children were required to reason at a level that explicitly recognises both their own and the others' representation of reality. For the children to have recognised that it was their own instructions that were inadequate in the situation they found themselves in required that they had achieved ToM. Research in ToM has shown that a range of communicative experiences and social interactions provide prerequisites for the children's intellectual development from early perception, to interpretation, and to the conceptual understanding of others. But our findings and analysis suggest that the introduction of CCTV technology is incapable of encouraging ToM on its own. The extant research suggests that it will only be where some form of cognitive apprenticeship has already been provided by a peer, family member or some 'significant other' that the child will be capable of making use of communications technology of this kind.

As Donaldson (1978) demonstrated, children's capabilities have often been underestimated in clinical studies where tasks were given that made no sense to them. It might be thought that this was precisely what we were doing in this study. Yet video conferencing and CCTV provides a technology that most adults also find it difficult to adjust to. One only needed to observe our attempts as researchers using the CCTV (or in video conferencing) to gain each other's attention by direct appeal to the screen rather than to the camera to be convinced of this!

Donaldson's major contribution was to show that children's intellectual capability develops as they gain greater confidence and competence in finding meaning, and thus practical understanding, of the new contexts and situations in which they find themselves. Just as family and siblings may support individual children in developing their ToM through the zone of proximal development, so too can the early educator by providing supportive scaffolding. This scaffolding may include the organisation of interactive games and routines, and as we have shown, it may also include introducing associated new technologies.

In the early years play is considered a 'leading activity' (Leontiev, 1981, Oerter, 1993), and it should therefore be seen as a driving force in children's development of new forms of motivation and action. Play and imitation are primary contexts for representational and symbolic behaviour, and role play is therefore central to the processes of learning in the early years. As we have argued elsewhere (Siraj-Blatchford, 2004) and as van Oers (1999) has suggested, when children consciously reflect upon the relationship between their 'pretend' signs and 'real' meanings they are engaged in a form of semiotic activity that is a valuable precursor to new learning activities (p278). In discussing the transition from play to learning activity Carpay and van Oers (1993) argue that:

> ...learning activity must be fostered as a new special form of play activity. As a new quality emerging from play activity, it can be argued that learning activity has to be conceived as a *language game* in which negotiation about meanings in a community of learners is the basic strategy for the acquisition of knowledge and abilities. (cited in van Oers 1999, p273, author's emphasis)

This approach is implicit in emergent literacy and numeracy practices where educators specifically encourage children to recognise the value of using symbols to represent and quantify artefacts. A great deal can be done to promote these processes in the wider play context and new forms of play might usefully be developed in applying the new technologies. In the case of CCTV the most obvious developments might include the encouragement of more structured and scaffolded play, based upon the use of TV in the children's favourite programmes – such as the Tellytubbies.

Image 10

The trials have continued at Gamesley Early Excellence Centre (Image 10) where they have found that the CCTV system provides children with a play environment that enhances their communication, language and literacy.

e-mail

Some e-mail applications were developed and evaluated in the Kinderet project, where Outlook Express was used to promote communication between children from different pre-schools in Portugal. There are many ways of sending and receiving email without using Outlook Express. Your internet service provider may provide you with a mail service but one of the most popular alternatives is Microsoft's Hotmail (www.hotmail.com). The services provided by Hotmail, Yahoo (http://mail.yahoo.com) and Google's Gmail (http://gmail.google.com) are all accessed from the web browser, so have the advantage of being accessible from any computer on the World Wide Web. None of these services were developed for children and most of the interfaces are not at all child friendly. This means the children will need quite a bit of support, but it is worth the effort. The Magic Desktop recently released by EasyBits (http://www.easybits.com) provides a means by which you can choose (on start-up) to run a computer with its regular desktop or provide children with their own more appropriate and secure graphical interface, which includes email. A major advantage of this technology is that its email system and internet browser allows the children to access only the email addresses and Websites you have entered into the system in advance.

In one Northamptonshire school we learned how children had worked with the teacher's parents when they went on a cruise. In collaboration with the children, the teacher set up a pretend ship's bridge to support socio-dramatic play. The children followed the ship's progress through the P&O website, and received email updates from the voyagers. The children wrote to them asking about their voyage. Such experiences have great potential for enriching the educational experience of the children. (*Marie Folland, Julie Oxlade, Ecton Brook School, Northamptonshire*)

Image 11 shows the P&O site that the children were browsing, and Image 12 the ship's 'bridge', which provided a prop for socio-dramatic play.

Images 11 and 12

Veronica Carter has been using email with her 4-5 year old Reception Class at Camelsdale First School in West Sussex for several years.

As Veronica says:

> The key to its success is that the children are communicating with people that they genuinely want to communicate with, and who genuinely want to communicate with them. Messages are sent and received from mums and dads, grannies and granddads and uncles and aunts. Everybody gets a turn because we can always arrange for older siblings or friends in school to send a message or have the Head write to the class and one of the children who does not get messages from home can be the one to reply. A lot of parents have access to email at work even if they don't have it at home and using it from work does not seem to be a problem for them.

Veronica provides many applications of email on her school website (which is well worth a visit) and her suggestions include:

- Encourage the families of class members to email the class periodically.
- Use email within your school, between classes etc.
- When visitors come to your class/school, or when the class goes on an educational visit, send thank you emails with some follow-up questions.
- Keep in email contact with relatives/friends of the children travelling abroad and use this to find out more about other countries.
- Email Father Christmas.

Veronica Carter

http://www.camelsdale.w-sussex.sch.uk/youvegotmail.asp

Socio-dramatic play

In this chapter we have explored some possibilities for supporting communication and collaboration with ICT. But it is socio-dramatic play that provides the most powerful context for this in early childhood. What practitioners need more than anything are the resources to exploit this pedagogy more effectively. This requires software developers to produce more, and better, role play software, and it also requires the rest of us to be doing more to disseminate good practice and provide supporting guidance. Resources are slowly becoming available. An excellent example of what is required in the way of support has been produced by Maggie Wagstaff, Advisory Teacher for IT and SEN in Warwickshire, who has developed a range of materials to support ICT and Role play in Early Years Settings. The use of Brilliant Computing's 'At the Vet's' (see Image

13) has already been referred to; and Maggie has suggested the following possible extensions:

At the Vet's:

- Weighing the pets, use an electronic scales and toy animals!
- Make an appointment sheet
- Make Pet record cards, Battersea dogs' home website is very useful http://www.dogshome.org
- Labels for pills and medicines
- Use a Cash till for the bills
- Use a painting package to make identity discs
- Make and use tape recordings of animal noises
- Use a microphone to call the next animal for the vet to see. Remember a microphone can be used with sound recorder on your computer
- Take digital photos and use the negative effect in Photo editor to get an X-Ray effect
- Make an 'Animals for sale' board with digital photos on display
- Use the bordered paper effect in 2Simple, 2 Publish to make the 'For sale' or 'lost and found' notices
- Look for thermometers and stethoscopes, which give some feedback e.g. digital reading on thermometer

Image 13

Charts printed off and made from a spreadsheet give children the opportunity to tabulate and offer open opportunity to collect whatever information they decide is appropriate

Blank paper is also useful!

On the CD there are printable examples of many different kinds of paper, pet disc example, Battersea dogs home data, pill labels, animal noises. You will nee the program used to make the examples to open the files eg Textease

The talking element of software is very useful in all role play. A Clicker Grid of animal pictures would allow children to press the animal and hear the word, as well as choose the order for the animals to see the vet. Similarly with Text ease, a word bank with pictures and the voice recorded sound of their name would individualise this process.

(Maggie Wagstaff)

Note

1 For more information see http://www.datec.org.uk

3

Creativity and Learning to Learn

We have seen that a good way to understand the development of young children's creativity is to consider it in terms of the development and manipulation of 'schemes'. To be creative we need two things:

- Knowledge of a broad range of alternative things that can be done, or thought – that is, a range of possible schemes

- The playful disposition to try schemes out in new contexts, in the mind's eye or in the material world

In her recent review of the research, Sandra Russ (2003) suggests that play not only reflects the cognitive and affective processes that are important in creativity but it also supports the development of creative capability. Although she argues that our understanding of the specific cognitive and affective abilities or dispositions involved remains unclear, she maintains that:

> There is a large body of studies that have found relations between play processes and creativity. Most of these studies either looked at play in a global fashion or investigated cognitive processes in play. A smaller body of studies, including my own, has found relations between affective processes in play and creativity as well.

Sylva *et al* (1976) and Vandenberg (1980) have also shown that play facilitates problem solving. Divergent thinking is central to both play and creativity, and longitudinal studies have also shown that creativity in pretend play is predictive of divergent thinking over time (Clark *et al*,1989, Russ *et al*, 1999). As Edwards and Hiler (1993) argued in their *Teacher's guide to Reggio Emilia*, we should encourage young children in their day-to-day practices of *analysis* (e.g. seeing similarities and differences); *synthesis* (e.g. rearranging, reorganising); and *evaluation* (e.g. judging the value of things). Young children are developmentally capable of all these high level thinking skills. And as Edwards and Hiler point out, young children benefit from meaningful open-ended discussions and the benefits of curriculum integration through investigation or topic based projects are often considerable. In supporting their creativity, we should encourage children to:

- look playfully for alternative ways of doing things
- see that there is always a choice
- make connections between things
- make unusual comparisons
- see things from the points of view of others

Perhaps most importantly, we should be provocative in our interactions with young children and keep asking them: '*what if...?*' There is immense potential in ICT applications that offer the possibility of open ended decision making and problem solving. To take a concrete example, Babyz (Mindscape) offers an entirely open-ended play environment featuring 'virtual life' babies who need to be fed when they are hungry, put to bed Images 14 and

when they are tired. They can be given toys to play with, tickled to make them laugh, and comforted when they are anxious (Image 14). The use of this software, supported as required by an adult, can be integrated with socio-dramatic play activities in the home corner and in outdoor play. By contrast, the transport problem solving environment offered by Fisher Price's *Learning in Toyland* Fliptrack would be more difficult to integrate and has only one solution (Image 15).

Computer based simulations and adventure games provide powerful contexts for supporting creativity, especially when they are integrated across the curriculum and when the adult takes on the role of a partner in the play. Edwards and Hiler (1993) describe this role:

> The adult role in these activities is to provide material and intellectual support and guidance and to act as partners to the children in the process of discovery and investigation... They take their cues from children through careful listening

and observation, and know when to encourage risk-taking and when to refrain from interfering.

Smilansky (1968) was one of the first researchers to demonstrate that teachers could teach play skills. Smilansky was particularly concerned about the relatively poor play skills of many children from low socio-economic status (SES) backgrounds and she worked with the children for 90 minutes a day, five days a week, over nine weeks. The adults supported the children's play by making comments and suggestions and giving demonstrations. As a result of these interventions the children's cognitive abilities significantly improved in comparison with those who received no such support. Smilansky (1968, 1990) has shown that socio-dramatic play can enhance the development of children's creativity, social skills and language development.

When negotiating play scenarios and in their ongoing co-ordination of roles, children have to recognise and respond to different ideas and perspectives. In collaboratively assigning particular pretend functions to an object they engage in cognitive decentering. The competences they develop will provide the basis for their coordination of cognitive perspectives with learning partners and teachers when they go to school. In Chapter 2 we cited van Oers' (1999) argument that reflecting upon the relationship between pretend signs and real meanings will help children to prepare for their transition to primary school. The importance of such metacognitive processes should not be underestimated. In 2004 the UK Minister for School Standards commissioned a report to clarify the concept of learning to learn. The working group of leading academics and headteachers argued in their final report:

> [Although] the more precise specification of the family of practices that constitute learning to learn must await both further psychological re-search and educational developments, we are for the present convinced that a very important or senior member of the family, one we regard as at the core of learning to learn, is *metacognition*... Much of what teachers do in helping students to learn how to learn consists of strengthening their meta-cognitive capacity, namely the capacity to monitor, evaluate, control and change how they think and learn. This is a critical feature of personalised learning. (Hargreaves *et al*, 2005)

Personalised learning remains a contested term. In his response to a question about the implications of individualised learning pathways for the primary sector addressed to BECTA's '*ICT advice for teachers: Ask an Expert*' site, Peter Humphreys of *Personalised Education Now* outlined the basic principles of personalisation:

> The ramifications for the primary sector I believe will be a shift in emphases from teaching to learning, from content to learning to learn, and the notion of learner as researcher. ...We need not feel at sea with such agendas as personalisation. The best of early years practice has long been consistent with many of these ideals and practitioners have maintained and developed those motivations and predispositions of the young that set them apart from those that are weary and disengaged later in their learning. (Humphreys, 2005)

Humphreys here identifies one of the major motivations for developing greater personalisation, a concern to support inclusion and the development of positive dispositions to learning. These issues are taken up in Chapter 4. Another of the key ideas (DfES, 2003) is that digital portfolios of an individual's learning may ultimately be applied to support the processes of transition throughout lifelong learning. Digital portfolios have been trialled at various levels of education but examples of their use in the early years remain scarce. Two recent examples of good practice from Northamptonshire reception classes are included in Appendix A.

There is strong evidence that computers can be applied to help even young children think about thinking, and that the ICT applications that support the development of metacognition and learning to learn are also those that most effectively support communication and collaboration and socio-dramatic play. But as the editors of *New Perspectives for Learning*, and Agalianos (2003) have reported, numerous research programmes across Europe have now demonstrated that in the compulsory school sector:

> ...the availability of technology alone cannot bring about radical change
>
> ...while some (potentially effective) technologies are embraced (by educators) others are resisted
>
> The use of technology in classrooms is found to be socially contextualised, interacting with the institutional and organisational cultures of schools and reflecting elements of the prevailing social relations in and around the context of use, (PJB Associates, 2003)

We shouldn't be surprised by any of this. An educational tool or technology is a commercial product and, just like any other product in the marketplace, it will only be of value when it is fit for its purpose. That is, when the assumptions and values of its producers are congruent with those of its end users (in this case educators and young children). Unfortunately, this has often not been true in educational technology. In the early years particularly, the pedagogical assumptions made by the software developers were often inappropriate. Most early childhood educators across Europe promote child-centred practices that prioritise the development of children's emergent awareness and positive dispositions towards learning. Yet this has often stood in stark contrast to the drill and practice or programmed learning approach that characterised the educational software available.

On no account should we treat the technology currently on offer as any kind of 'irreducible brute fact' (Nobel, 1979). Young children deserve better than that. We should instead encourage early years practitioners to make their own critical evaluations of what is on offer, to be critical consumers, and to adapt only the best of the available technology to their particular needs. At the same time we should encourage the maximum engagement of teachers and children in the ongoing practice of technological design (van Leeuwen, 2004). The alternative will be to end up in the ridiculous and ironic situation described by the originator of the C++ programming language:

> I have always wished for a computer that would be as easy to use as my telephone. My wish came true. I no longer know how to use my telephone. (attributed to Bjarne Stronstrup)

Throughout this book we have used the term 'application' in its broadest sense to include all the means by which various technological artefacts and products come to be applied in early learning environments. Our focus has been on the situated educational use of each ICT tool rather than simply on one particular hardware or software product. This is because we believe that good applications should always be seen as the product of educational *practitioners* – however well their efforts may be supported by the particular hardware and software they use. When we share exemplars of good practice we need to consider both the technology and the specific use that it is made of it. Unfortunately most published reviews of educational software fail to acknowledge this principle. This is especially important in a context where many authorities have expressed disappointment over the slow progress of integrating ICT into education.

Too often ICT has been seen as something just to be bolted onto existing educational practices, rather than to transform them. The importance of integration was mentioned in Chapter 1 as one characteristic of the best applications identified in the DATEC research. We included an application's potential in terms of integration in our *Application Review Proforma* (see Appendix B) which has provided practitioners with a basic framework to apply in sharing their best practice. But while many pre-school settings now recognise the need to integrate ICT across the curriculum, there is often less emphasis on integrating the computer in pedagogical terms. The term 'integration' needs to be understood as relating to the way in which ICT is incorporated into student learning. As Cox *et al*, (2003) have argued, the research evidence suggests that the extent to which ICT contributes to educational attainment in schools: '... *depends on the way in which the teacher selects and organises ICT resources, and how this use is integrated into other activities in the classroom and beyond*' (Cox *et al*, 2003).

Yet integration continues to be understood almost exclusively in terms of curriculum subjects rather than pedagogic practices, and this will need to change if we are to see progress.

While generic open-ended problem-solving and simulation applications appear to offer children the greatest screen-based opportunities for supporting integrated learning and development today, programmable toys may ultimately offer even greater potential.

Programmable toys

Well-designed on-screen applications support creativity by providing for a wide variety of possible responses by the children. Programmable toys may provide still greater possibilities. Many of the benefits gained from older pupils using Logo, identified in Becta's (2003) *Research Briefing for ICT in Mathematics*, will be paralleled by young children's use of programmable toys. Problem-solving skills will be encouraged and geometric concepts, collaboration, and higher level thinking developed. Clements (1994) has long advocated Logo. In an early study (Clements and Gullo, 1984), involving 6 year olds in a range of activities over three months, gains were found as measured by both the *Torrance Test of Creative Thinking* and a test of reflectivity, which were not matched by the control group. Significantly, Clements and Gullo also found improvements in children's metacognition and their ability to describe a route on a map verbally.

In programming a toy to behave in a certain way, children have to see the problem from the toy's perspective. They have to decentre, adopting a body-centred system of reference which Papert (1980) termed 'body syntonicity'. In 2004, at *Earls Barton School* in Northamptonshire a Reception Teacher worked with her pupils in developing a diorama of their

Image 16

village (Image 16) featuring all its prominent buildings, shops and amenities. The children then programmed Pixie (Swallow Systems) to deliver letters to different shops:

After carrying out the activity with the children I feel that it was very successful. All the children contributed even those who very rarely speak in a whole class situation and using pixie held their concentration. The activity began to develop the children's problem solving as they were having to estimate and edit their decisions. It is interesting to observe the children when they are using Pixie, as some children can visualise where Pixie needs to go and will just enter the directions, while other children will have to walk the route Pixie will take before entering the instructions. (Claire Hately, Earls Barton School)

In another Northamptonshire classroom, children worked in groups of five, taking turns at making their Roamer (Valiant Technology) dance. The children squealed in delight as Roamer (Image 17) began to move and they became very excited by its changing directions. The teacher then asked the children to write down their own dance routines for Roamer and to programme them in. They wrote on whiteboards so they could rub out and edit, and found Roamer easy enough to operate to programme their ideas independently. In the process, the children used a variety of forms of mark making to record their instructions (Image 18).

Image 17

Image 18

Later the children worked in pairs to write dance routine programmes for Roamer. They worked in pairs to negotiate and plan a dance and they were given a variety of musical instruments to create accompanying music for Roamer to perform their dance to. This time the children worked on paper and their programmes were stuck into a scrap book which we called 'Roamer's Dance Book'....At last I have found a resource that gives the children a real and concrete reason for recording their ideas in writing – in order to remember instructions they need to write them down in some way. The children wanted to do this so that they could remember their dance ideas rather than just because the teacher had told them to write. High levels of well being and involvement all round. Lots of negotiation, verbalised thinking and cooperation.' (Chrissie Dale, King's Sutton School)

As Fine and Thornbury (1998) have argued:

> Our experience in using control in the early years is that children talk and listen, revise and review, and evaluate and refine the use of their language in order to be understood and to achieve their joint goals.

A wide range of 'intelligent' toys have entered the domestic market in recent years and some of these toys have been found to support collaboration (Luckin *et al*, 2003). A great many research questions arise, but one significant feature of many of these toys is that their behaviour has been programmed to 'develop' as they appear to learn from their play with the child. Often the 'learning' is more apparent than real but the effects that play of this kind might have on children is worthy of greater research attention. Meanwhile, our knowledge of toys that are effective is growing but more needs to be done to support practitioners in developing strategies for their application.

A significant advantage of programmable toys such as Swallow System's Pixie and the Technology Teaching System's Bee-Bot's is that the simplicity of the interface provided supports young children in quickly learning to programme them. DATEC found that most of the best applications provided this sort of transparency: their functions were clearly defined and intuitive. A good example of this is the drag and drop facility of a modern computer desktop. Functional transparency is also exemplified in the Sony Mavica digital camera that saves images on a floppy disk. After taking a photograph, children can remove the disk with the photo on it and put it into the computer. They can double click on a floppy disc (desktop shortcut) icon, and then double-click on the thumbnail image to open the picture on the screen. Digital camera design has improved in recent years and we now see a wide range of effective applications being developed in pre-schools, where many practitioners have extended the work to include the use of presentation tools such as PowerPoint and even interactive whiteboards.

Image 19

Digital images

After they developed PowerPoint presentations about various activities associated with Divali, a group of children at another Northamptonshire school used a digital camera to take photographs of each other in their Nativity play costumes. The teacher (Julie Williams) then imported the images into *Present*, a simple PowerPoint type programme in 'Tizzy's First Tools'. She observed:

I worked with a small group of children using this programme on the interactive whiteboard. Through discussion the children selected photographs. Children took turns in using the whiteboard pen to select, drag and resize the images. They then decided on captions for the images which I typed for them. Valuable discussion on sequencing ensued when one child pointed out 'You can't have the shepherds first because Mary and Joseph have to go to Bethlehem first.' Again the white board pen was used to order the slides in the correct sequence. I was amazed by the speed with which the children grasped the idea of the drag and drop facility and were able to resize and reorder the Images.

The children's reactions to the Divali PowerPoint were entirely positive. They derive enormous pleasure from recognising themselves and their friends in the photographs and the images prompt memories which are very valuable for language development. ...Some of their comments undoubtedly reveal an awareness and understanding of the festival of Divali which was not present before the project began. (Julie Williams, Bozeat Primary School)

Many early years practitioners have also found that the immediacy of the images produced by a digital camera are of great value. As the Reception teacher in another Northamptonshire school said:

I believe that the digital camera provided the activity with more focus; because the children were taking their own pictures, they seemed to be looking more carefully for things to photograph. Most could provide an explanation of why they were choosing to take a particular shot and those who could not were given the opportunity to do so when we were viewing the images upon our return to the classroom. Most did this. In this way, I feel that the camera helped to clarify and consolidate the children's learning. (Susan Grey, Rowlett Primary School)

A number of teachers refer to the value of digital cameras in providing instant visual feedback:

For one little boy in my class in particular, with special needs, it was a powerful tool to use to value his presence in the group. I used photographs to identify children's name cards, and put my own photograph on the back of my chair, which gave everyone a strong message of acceptance within the group. I took lots of photographs of the children involved in activities to display strategically in different areas, as it records the moment of learning in a tangible and accessible way. The children love to return to the images for referral and discussion with their parents and friends at frequent intervals, which encourages the sharing of ideas, and provides inspiration and stimuli for other activities.' (Sue Poole, Eastfield Primary School)

At All Saints Primary School in Northamptonshire, a digital camera was used to support the investigation of bean growth. The children recorded the growth and made up their own 'Bean Diary' to record their findings:

> The children loved using the cameras....They enjoyed looking at their images after they had taken it and decide whether to re-take or if they were content. The children recorded their own serial numbers of photographs for printing purposes. (Mia Hobbs, All Saints Primary School)

Image 20

PowerPoint

PowerPoint and other presentation tools are used frequently in Northamptonshire's Lead Reception classrooms (see Chapter 6). Useful applications of PowerPoint were also developed in both the English and in the Portuguese Kinderet contexts. As Veronica Carter (2005) has observed, with all the colour, movement and sounds they can produce; 'it should not have been a surprise to find out how appealing it was to four year olds!'

http://www.camelsdale.w-sussex.sch.uk/powerpoint_in_yr.asp

A wide range of possible applications are possible. For a taste it is worth trying some of the following PowerPoint resources (currently available for free download) from:

http://icteachers.co.uk/resources/resources_earlyyears.htm

■ for spelling some common words with B as the beginning sound (Bridgeen McNulty)

■ for recognising colours (Lorna Schembri)

■ supporting the teaching of basic arithmetic with a series of animated additions (Veronica Carter)

You can download a PowerPoint viewer from Microsoft at no cost. But note – the PowerPoint viewer is a viewer only and applications cannot be edited or changed with this tool. Presentation tools have of course been criticised:

> One of the criticisms that's been raised about PowerPoint is that it can give the illusion of coherence and content when there really isn't very much coherence or content,' said Edward Miller, an education researcher

and board member of the Alliance for Childhood, which advocates limited use of computer technology in early childhood education. (Glasner, 2002)

And, as Peter Norvig (2004) has suggested, at their worst, PowerPoint presentations offer; 'a world with almost no pronouns or punctuation. A world where any complex thought must be broken into seven-word chunks, with colourful blobs between them'. Norvig cites Cliff Nass in arguing that although PowerPoint may allow some main points to be communicated 'even if the speaker mumbles, forgets, or is otherwise grossly incompetent... it makes it harder to have an open exchange between presenter and audience, to convey ideas that do not neatly fit into outline format, or to have a truly inspiring presentation.' (*op cit*).

Interactive whiteboards (IWBs)

We know of no systematic research into the use of either PowerPoint or interactive whiteboards in early years classrooms but some particularly positive practices have been observed. Often these involve individuals or small groups of children using the IWB independently to operate a wide range of software including *Leaps and Bounds* (Granada Learning) and *Izzy's Island* (Sherston). In our opinion the technology also has great potential for adults working with groups on focused tasks or in exploring adventure games and simulations they could not otherwise operate for developmental reasons – such as interface sophistication or reading capability (Image 22). We noted that practitioners often find the initial demonstration of software on an IWB a very effective introduction.

mages 21 and 22

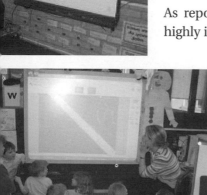

As reported in Chapter 7, the IWBs were valued extremely highly in the Northamptonshire reception classes, and similar findings have been reported in the school based applications cited by Mirandanet (2005). Their IWB case studies showed:

The use of interactive adventure games (such as Civilizations) on an interactive whiteboard means that students can work as a team. Not only do these group activities reinforce Literacy skills, but they also develop the wider Key Skills of Problem Solving, Working with Others and Improving Own Learning and Performance. (Mirandanet, 2005)

But the Mirandanet materials also urge caution, and it is argued that whole-class use of IWBs has both positive and negative effects:

> It promotes pupils' debates and helps them visualise difficult concepts and processes. However, some teachers focus only on the presentation aspects, disregarding the use of simulations and modelling which might be more challenging for the pupils. (*op cit*)

The introduction of IWBs has coincided with national literacy and numeracy initiatives in UK schools that have promoted interactive whole class teaching. As Tanner *et al* (2005) point out, this was not an attempt to return to more traditional approaches:

> It is not achieved by adopting a simplistic formula of 'drill and practice' and lecturing the class, or by expecting pupils to teach themselves from books. It is a two-way process in which pupils are expected to play an active part by answering questions, contributing points to discussion, and explaining and demonstrating their methods to the class. (DfEE, 2001, 1.26)

Unfortunately IWBs are only interactive when they are applied by educators using an interactive pedagogy, and most of the evidence so far suggests that this may not be happening in schools (Hargreaves *et al*, 2003, Smith *et al*, 2004). As Tanner *et al* (2005) argue, the frequency of teacher questioning has increased, but this has not resulted in more sustained shared thinking:

> Most pupil responses remain very short, with an average length of five seconds and involving three or four words in 70 per cent of cases (Smith *et al*, 2004: 408). Teachers tend to evaluate rather than extend or build on pupils' responses to questions (Mroz *et al*, 2000). Sustained interactions with individuals and pupil utterances of more than ten words are extremely rare (Burns and Myhill, 2004: 44; Hargreaves *et al*, 2003: 233). (Tanner *et al*, 2005)

The REPEY study (Siraj-Blatchford *et al*, 2002) looked at the proportion of open and closed questions being used by adults in the effective pre-school settings identified by the EPPE study (Sylva *et al*, 2004). A total of 1,967 adult questions were analysed. Closed questions may be rhetorical and are usually applied to elicit short, factual answers; open questions, by contrast, are those that Galton *et al* (1999) and Alexander (2000) refer to as stimulating 'higher-order' thinking; where answers are not necessarily pre-determined and more than one possible answer exists. While the Oracle study in 1996 identified 34.6 per cent of all Key Stage 2 primary school teacher questions as 'closed' and 9.9 per cent as 'open', it is not encouraging that the REPEY study found even less open ended questioning by the pre-school educators (5.1 per cent). As a tool, the IWB does support whole-class teaching and in the absence of specific training their introduction into early childhood settings may therefore serve to reduce rather than improve interactivity. As Tanner *et al* (2005) maintain, further research is needed. They quote Beauchamp (2004):

> In the early stages of use, the IWB is treated typically as a black/whiteboard substitute and serves to reinforce traditional pedagogies as teachers pass through a period of de-skilling and technological vulnerability. During this period interaction is often reduced as teachers restrict the use of the board to themselves, sometimes expressing concern that pupils might put the board into a state that they would not be able to undo due to technical ignorance. (Beauchamp, 2004)

Another important issue relates to the installation of IWBs. In many cases the IWBs in Northamptonshire Reception classes were installed too high up for the children to operate them independently. Image 23 shows a child using an Oxford Reading Tree (Sherston) talking story. Image 24 shows that some of the controls provided in *2Simple's* 2Go screen turtle are out of reach. The positioning of the boards in Northamptonshire was subsequently corrected, either by lowering the boards, sometimes requiring some customisation of the projector cradles, or by providing staging for the children to stand on.

Images 23 and 24

There appears to be no specific expert advice on the safety of using the projectors associated with front lit IWBs with children under 5. BECTA currently provides advice which includes warnings of a potential risk to eyesight but it is not clear whether the risks for young children are the same as for older children:

> It's important to be aware of the health and safety implications of using projection equipment such as interactive whiteboards in the classroom, particularly if children might stand in front of the beam to give presentations to the rest of the class. All projectors, if misused, have the potential to cause eye injury; so some simple guidelines should be followed:

- Make clear to all users that no one should stare directly into the beam of the projector.
- When entering the beam, users should not look towards the audience for more than a few seconds.
- Encourage users to keep their backs to the projector beam.
- Children should be supervised at all times when a projector is being used.

A maximum of 1,500 ANSI lumens is normally adequate for projection equipment in most classroom environments. The only exception might be extreme ambient lighting conditions. In this case the advice is to use window blinds rather than increasing the brightness of the projector.

When purchasing or using a projector for purposes when it is likely that a person will be standing in front of the beam, consider using a method of brightness reduction, such as a neutral density filter or brightness adjustment facility. These modifications can be removed or adjusted for other purposes such as cinema projections, when no one will be standing in front of the beam, allowing the projector to be used to its full potential. (Becta, 2005)

The projector currently featured by Research Machines as the best buy is capable of delivering 2,000 ANSI lumens and numerous 3,000 lumen models are currently on the market for less than £1,000. More expensive projectors designed for use in lecture halls are rated up to 10,000 lumens. While the concerns about the safety of front lit interactive whiteboards therefore remain unresolved, alternatives include the use of – albeit more expensive – 'rear projection' interactive whiteboards and LCD touch screens.

The importance of interactivity

Vygotsky identified the critical role of verbal interaction in early learning thus: '...*the true direction of the development of thinking is not from the individual to the social but from the social to the individual.*'

More recently, Alexander (2004) has cited research from developmental psychology, neuroscience and socio-linguistic research as well as a range of classroom studies to present 'Dialogic Teaching' as an approach that:

> ...demands both pupil engagement *and* teacher intervention. And the principle means by which pupils actively engage and constructively intervene is through talk. (Alexander, 2004, authors' emphasis)

As Alexander notes, this account of dialogic teaching resonates with Bruner's 'mutualist and dialectical pedagogy', Gordon Wells' 'dialogic enquiry', Mercer's 'interthinking', and Lindfor's 'dialogue of enquiry' (p18 *op cit*). Each of these also provides valuable classroom extensions of the principles developed to encourage 'sustained shared thinking' in pre-school learning environments (Dowling, 2005).

Alexander (2004) observes that of all the talk strategies that educators draw upon 'discussion and scaffolded dialogue have by far the greatest cognitive potential' (p24), but that these demand the greatest skill and subject knowledge from school teachers. He makes the point that school teachers tend to stick to rote, recitation and exposition for reasons of security: '*They make it unlikely that awkward questions about evidence, truth and opinion will interrupt the flow of information from teacher to taught*' (p24 *op cit*).

For primary, and secondary, school teachers teaching discrete curriculum subjects although they have no specialist training, these anxieties are to be expected. But anxieties of this kind have no place in early years practice. Regardless of the teaching context, for teachers to be fearful of pupils' questions suggests that they believe that they *should* always know the answer. But there are many reasons to reject this assumption at any levels of education such as:

- the practical impossibility for any teacher to know everything
- the need for teachers to model and share the challenge, excitement and processes of learning
- the fact that ICT has greatly improved our access to information, with the consequence that the skill of recall becomes less important
- the fact that knowledge is growing and changing at a rate that makes it impossible for any individual to keep up with anything more than a closely defined specialist subject
- the need, in the light of the above, to encourage children to improve their information skills, to 'learn to learn', and to accept and embrace the inevitability of life-long learning

Alexander emphasises the importance of subject knowledge because he believes that the process of teaching dialogically in the later years of schooling demands a 'clear conceptual map' of the direction the pupils' thinking should take. At the pre-school stage, and throughout the early years, where the emphasis is on processes and dispositions rather than subject knowledge, the curriculum 'conceptual map' should be seen as an emergent one, and the educational priority should be on the adults providing positive role models as learners themselves continuing, collaboratively, to learn to learn.

This argument should not be taken to imply that a strong and broad general education is not important when preparing early childhood educators. Quite the reverse: the intellectual demands of children's questions can be considerable. Some examples were compiled and answered in a series run in Nursery World in 1999-2000 (and in Siraj-Blatchford and MacLeod-Brudenell, 1999). The questions were all open to investigation, for instance:

Why are bubbles round?

Why are some people black and other people white?

Why don't birds get an electric shock when they perch on power lines?

Why is the sky blue?

Why is it cold?... and why do I shiver?

It is only in academic work at a graduate level that most of us develop sufficient information skills to tackle such questions, and it is often only at this point in our education that we become aware of competing knowledge claims.

The benefits of adopting a process-based and open-ended approach to the curriculum in early childhood are not restricted to the children alone, as Lynn Kennington, headteacher at the Gamesley Early Excellence Centre (see Chapter 6) has argued:

> What a head or a leader should do is let people fly and give them the wings to do it. They should develop people individually, let people take their ideas off on tangents and see where it takes them. Because people develop creatively that way, and they are more fulfilled as teachers. (Lynn Kennington, 2005)

4

Social Inclusion and the
Digital Divide

In Chapter 3 we identified the role of personalisation in supporting inclusion. Two teachers in Northamptonshire produced reflective accounts of their recent ICT work in Rowan Gate special school. Julia Coles used *Clicker 4* (Crick Software) to provide a structure her pupils with speech, language and communication disorders could build upon in order to achieve successful writing outcomes(Image 25): 'For children with Autism the most successful activities are those which provide visual prompts and a scaffold for them to work on. Clicker 4 also works on this premise'.

Image 25

Julia intends building upon the successes she has had with the tool to develop a wide range of grids:

If we have a means of providing our children with the tools to 'write' then I think we should embrace it and empower our children... I believe that in comparison with other established and alternative approaches to achieving the specified learning objectives Clicker 4 has shown itself capable of providing a motivating and successful means through which children with speech, language and communication disorders can write. It is a tool that I would not wish to be without. (Julia Coles, Rowan Gate School)

Carol Whiting, at the same school, built upon a series of 1:1 *Soundbeam* (Therminvox) sessions with a withdrawn, elective mute pupil. The soundbeam was used to encourage interaction, physically, emotionally and (possibly) verbally. *Soundbeam* provides synthesized music and combined sounds through the breaking of a beam. Image 26 shows the child's subsequent work with an interactive white board application (http://www.teaching time.co.uk/).

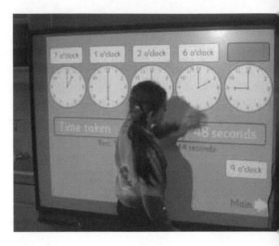

Following these applications of ICT the pupil's confidence has grown and her inhibitions have reduced. Most significantly she is now interacting:

Image 26

> Overall with the use of the interactive white board and the soundbeam, B appears to be less inhibited... sustained progress has been made not only for B, but the rest of the class too.

Home learning, parent partnership and the role of ICT

Chapter 3 mentions using digital portfolios to support the personalisation of learning. Portfolios and displays are used in this way in many preschool settings to provide the sort of documentation popularised so effectively by Reggio Emilia (Siraj-Blatchford, 1999). Portfolios and displays are also used to inform and involve parents more closely in their children's education. As one of our respondents in Northamptonshire (see Chapter 7) observed:

> The digital camera, laptop and whiteboard have certainly helped parents to see more of the precious moments that might otherwise be lost to them, which has promoted lots of discussion with their children in the mornings. At the end of the year, I intend to transfer each child's file onto a CD, which will be given to parents as a memento of their child's first year at our school. In this way, I am able, as a Foundation Stage practitioner, to share with parents the remarkable achievements of their children. (Susan Grey, Rowlett School)

Research suggests that home-school communication leads to better understanding and more positive attitudes by teachers and parents about one another's roles and improves children's academic performance. We collected data on the home use of ICT in both our initial UK of KidSmart and the European extension study (Siraj-Blatchford and

Siraj-Blatchford, 2002a, 2004a). Data related to the home ICT experiences of children in Northamptonshire was collected in 2004.

In the early KidSmart study (see Chapter 6) 156 parent questionnaires were returned. We particularly wanted to check whether the initial level of ICT provision offered by the settings or any improvements, were related to the ICT provided in homes. We found no evidence of any connection. In this first study, 59 (53 per cent) of the parents reported that they had computers and 87 per cent said that their children had access to electronic toys in their homes, most commonly Barney, Furby, radio-controlled cars and electronic 'dogs'. It may have been significant that 67 of the parents who responded to the survey reported on boys and 44 on girls. We asked the parents who had computers what software they used with their children at home and they cited 75 different early learning and edutainment programmes! In this extraordinarily wide range the favourites, apart from Microsoft Paint and word processor packages, were:

The Tweenies (Nykris)
Learning Land (De Agostini UK)
The Jump Ahead Series (Havas)
Noddy (Tell Tale)
Thomas the Tank Engine and Friends

Amongst the numerous other titles mentioned were programmes produced by The Learning Company, Disney Interactive, Fisher Price and Dorling Kindersley. If nothing else, the variety of software titles referred to suggested that the parents might benefit from greater involvement in future pre-school developments.

Crook (2003) has argued there is a need to develop more applications that provide a continuity of educational experience between the home and the pre-school. His research shows a serious discontinuity at present, with little relevant software used and little parental involvement. Accordingly, we conducted a pilot study in two Cambridgeshire nurseries in 2003 to see what could be achieved. Parents in each nursery were invited to discuss how they might make the most of home computers in supporting their children's learning. Staff in both nurseries were pleased to note the high attendance of fathers and grandfathers at these events. The parents/carers were introduced to some of the research evidence and provided with a suite of Riverdeep software (donated by IBM) that was already being used in the settings. Practical activities were suggested for parents to support their children with the software. The parent/carers and nursery practitioners completed questionnaires and attended a follow up meeting later in the year to report on their progress. Both parent/carers and practitioners rated the project a great success. The schools' tacit endorsement of the software's educational value was important to the parents, who saw their children's enjoyment in an even more positive light:

> He sat down once with his granddad at the computer for five hours! The fact that the nursery uses the software makes you feel more confident that you didn't get some rubbish. (parent)

Given the small scale of the investigation it was inappropriate to measure specific learning outcomes but the nursery educators and the majority of the parents felt that their children had benefited. The results of this pilot study were clear: where parents are provided with the means to do so, they can and will significantly contribute to supporting their children. The key to this form of educational partnership seems to lie in the development of curriculum and pedagogic continuity between the home and the setting. The application of common computer software at home and in the nursery can be very productive. One way of achieving this, in the absence of funding, would be to use online software. As long as suitable internet filtering (or portal) software is installed, even the youngest children can benefit from the internet. In our opinion, it is best to purchase a product such as CyberDuck's *KidsWeb* (http://www.cyberd. co.uk/software/kidsweb.htm) or BrowserLock (http://www.Browser Lock.com) to create your own custom web portal. Both provide full Internet Explorer or other browser capability but restrict the links to only those websites you specify. Any other web address (url) entered into the browser is disallowed. BECTA (2004) also provides free foundation stage guidance on 'Using web-based resources' at: http://www.becta.org.uk/corporate/publications/documents/WBR_foundation.pdf

Research recently published by Buckingham and Scanlon (2004) identifies many of the barriers to learning that are unfortunately inherent in most edutainment software and websites. So it is essential to be severely discriminating in our choice of applications.

The home learning environment

The importance of the family to learning has been recognised for many years. Statistical analysis shows that mothers' qualification level and family socio-economic (SES) status are strong predictors of educational outcomes. But major research studies such as the *Effective Provision of Pre-school Education* (EPPE) project are now revealing the importance of the home learning environment (HLE) to early childhood development and learning. The EPPE research has shown that aspects of self-reported parental involvement in activities – such as reading to their child, teaching songs and nursery rhymes, playing with letters and numbers, visiting the library, painting and drawing, emphasising the alphabet – are significant positive influences which account for differences in attainment that are sustained well beyond pre-school. It is highly significant that this research also shows that these environmental factors are only moderately correlated with the mother's qualification level and family socio-economic status:

> These results suggest that policies for parents in disadvantaged communities which encourage active parenting strategies can help to promote young children's cognitive progress ... Many pre-schools already encourage parental participation, and some have developed programmes that feature parent education. The EPPE results indicate that programmes which directly promote activities for parents and children to engage in together are likely to be most beneficial for young children. (Sammons *et al*, 2002)

In the USA, the High/Scope Perry Pre-school Evaluation (Schweinhart and Weikart, 1997) and several other influential early childhood studies have shown the value of encouraging parents to contribute to the educational process. The value of parents and children reading books together at home has also been well established (Hewison, 1988). Many studies show that when parents, teachers and children collaborate towards the same goals this can improve academic performance across the curriculum (Siraj-Blatchford *et al*, 2003). Schools also report that children whose parents contribute to their education in the home show a more positive attitude towards learning and are better behaved in school (Hannon *et al*, 1990; Hewison, 1988).

Although detailed analysis of the effects of home ICT use was beyond the scope of the EPPE research, there are strong indications that when parents actively support their children at the computer and in other ICT contexts, similar benefits are likely. We know that young children ask more questions when they are involved in practical activities than when they are passive, and ICT provides one excellent such context. Computers also provide a means by which to support young children in their manipulation of symbols. Representations on the screen allow children to distance themselves from objects and this encourages verbal reflection and abstraction (Forman, 1984).

In their shared experience at the computer or in other ICT applications, an adult can draw the child's attention to their own learning and to themselves as learners, so developing metacognitive approaches. For example, an adult could draw attention to how a child has used a new skill or combined different materials or could recognise that children have concentrated, persevered or solved a problem (Wood 1988, Hohmann and Weikart 1995, Pramling 1990, QCA, 2000).

Moreover, adults and children can operate to advantage as co-players. Early childhood educators often suggest that adults should interact more with children in their play and stressed that adults need to be responsive and supportive to children's needs and potential in play situations, computer initiated or not. 'Interaction' is understood here as sustained involvement in an activity led predominantly by the child or children. 'Intervention' involves the input of new skills or knowledge to enable the play to continue to develop (Wood and Attfield 1997). Adults who interact with children in their play and adopt an 'extending' style which synchronises with the child's own intention, promote play as educationally profitable while valuing play in its own right (Tamburrini 1982).

> Commonplace interactive behaviour in the family is undervalued. Such behaviour has considerable potential for social learning in the early years. Even by arguing, a child can learn the implications of their actions. By discussing past and future events, a child can bring up their own memories, anxieties can be allayed, and they can reach an understanding of what has happened or might happen to them. (Tizard and Hughes 1988)

Researchers are now stressing the importance of parental involvement in children's computer use at home (Facer, 2002, Sanger, 1997, Giacquinta, Baucer and Levin, 1993). One of the most important findings has also been that the level of children's use of computers in school is directly influenced by their out of school experiences (Facer *et al*, 2000).

Giacquinta *et al* (1993) found that when children used home computers for educational purposes they were highly dependent on parental support. When children play games they usually play on their own. But Giacquinta *et al* found that the children who used home computers for educational purposes generally had parents who worked jointly with their children at the keyboard and offered praise as well as practical assistance:

Not only may the experience at home provide something not readily available in school but also it seems that the skills involved apply as much to the process of attention, perseverance, task performance and work organisation as to particular areas of knowledge. Learning how to learn may be as important as the specifics of what is learned. (Rutter, 1985)

Access to home computers

Our research provides information about parental attitudes towards the use of computers in early childhood. In the European KidSmart study the majority of parents were found to support the introduction of computers in the pre-school and at home (Siraj-Blatchford and Siraj-Blatchford, 2004a). But a surprising number (17 per cent) of German parents felt that computers had no place in the pre-school and 10 per cent were against their use at any stage of education. The KidSmart data cannot, however, be taken as representative of the overall population as it only relates to the experiences and attitudes of parents benefiting from the KidSmart initiative in disadvantaged communities (see Chapter 8).

We found that the proportion of KidSmart parents with computers at home tended to be somewhat higher than the national averages (OECD, 2001), but we felt that this was to be expected given the evidence that families with young children have more home computers than others (e.g. as reported in the PISA study). In the UK 60 per cent of KidSmart parents had a computer at home, in France the figure was 62 per cent and in Germany 88 per cent, but in Italy it was only 58 per cent and in Spain just 44 per cent. The pattern was complex, with major regional and urban-rural variations. In Italy for example, 83 per cent of the families living in the North (Legnago) had a computer at home, whereas in the centre (Benevento) this decreased to 43 per cent, and in the south (Catania) to only 39 per cent.

Table 2: Computer hardware and software used at home

Percentage	UK	Spain	Italy	Germany	France
Computer at home	60	44	58	88	62
Games software used	39	60	33	48	100
Internet/email used	23	17	20	30	40
Educational software	31	35	12	19	40
Supports employment	32	49	35	48	60

We also asked parents for specific information about the child's use of the computer at home:

Table 3

Percentage	UK	Spain	Italy	Germany	France
Child never uses	3	23	13	18	0
Child operates on his/her own	28	94	43	43	47
Child operates more than 5 hours per week	10	8	11	7	8

In our study of the home ICT experiences of reception class pupils in Northamptonshire (see Chapter 6), the sample included relatively few children from disadvantaged backgrounds, as most of the schools served populations of parents categorised as professional and skilled. Sixteen schools were included in our analysis:

Table 4

No. of parents completing questionnaires for schools	No. of parents	No. of boys' reported	No. of girls reported	Social class of parents
444 (86 per cent)	515	213	231	Mainly professional and skilled

The parents were asked whether they had a computer at home. Most did so (86 per cent), and those who said 'no' often qualified this by adding 'but we are about to get one' or something like 'she uses her Nan's computer and loves it.'

Our findings related to the home learning environment (in terms of what parents did with their children as defined from the EPPE research) showed how parents provide a home learning environment with support for the computer alongside reading, visits to the library, songs and nursery rhymes and playing with numbers and letters. The Northamptonshire parents reported on the frequency with which they supported their children with (see Table 5).

The table shows that most parents are very willing to share time with their children on basic literacy and numeracy tasks, but taking children to the library appears to be less popular and so does sharing time with them at the computer. This suggests that parents might benefit from

Table 5

'As a parent I...'	Never	Sometimes	Weekly	Daily
Read with my child	0	6	42	241
Take my child to the library	68	172	43	1
Sing songs and nursery rhymes with my child	7	63	99	105
Spend time at the computer with my child	39	110	105	24
Teach numbers and alphabet	2	25	100	130

guidance about the kind of engagement they might have with their child when they did so.

In line with our findings in other studies, the vast majority of Northamptonshire parents reported that their children used the computer for 1-3 hours per week, although a minority hardly ever used a computer, and a few used it in excess of 7 hours a week. The evidence suggests that these differences are unfortunately far from random. In our KidSmart research we found that while the children of higher socio-economic class (SES) families in the UK often use educational software, children in lower SES households use the home computers for playing games far more often. Figure 5 shows the distribution of time spent on the computer, drawn from a sample of 261 UK KidSmart parents. It shows a median usage of around 2 hours per week but 20 per cent of children spent 5 or more hours on the computer and most were from working class families. This

Figure 5

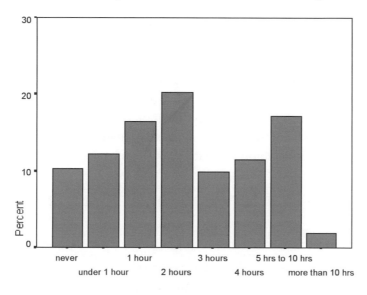

time child uses computer per week

was true of all the children who spent 10 hours or more per week on the computer.

In terms of the use made of the computer, games and entertainment were more popular (204 mentions), than educational user (164).

Russell and Stafford's (2002) survey also identified different patterns of use on socio-economic lines, with people of A and B social groups more likely to use computers for e-mail, the internet and work, while lone parents and unemployed council tenants more likely to be using the internet for 'playing/downloading games, seeking information about sports, chat rooms, and listening to/downloading music'. A recent US study on home computer use (Rathbun and West, 2003) found that the purposes computers were used for at home also varied according to children's sex, ethnicity, and SES. Children from higher SES families were more likely to use home computers for educational purposes and:

> White children with home computer access were more likely than Hispanic and Asian/Pacific Islander kindergartners to use them to play with educational programs, and more likely than Black or Hispanic kindergartners to use them for art or drawing programs. (Rathbun and West, 2003)

As McPake *et al* (2004) found, the degree of ICT competence children acquire in the home depends on a number of factors, including access to equipment, support for learning to use it, and the particular interests and aptitudes of older family members. There is little research into assessing any educational value gained by using poor quality edutainment and games software with young children but the effects are likely to be very similar to that of television viewing, about which we have quite a lot of evidence. We know, for example, that parents who watch a great deal of TV tend to have children who do the same, and excessive TV viewing is associated with family and peer difficulties (Comstock 1991). But if parents watch TV with their children and engage in joint conversation, they help them understand what they see. Thus, parent-child co-viewing results in:

- parents being able to raise questions about the realism of information

- parents assisting children in making sense of the story line

- parents expressing disapproval of negative on screen behaviour and commercial messages – teaching children to evaluate content rather than accept it uncritically.

When parents make an effort, pre-schoolers watch less TV, and find educational TV more appealing. They also watch programmes more often *with* their parents (Comstock 1991). This is likely to apply equally to computer use and in both cases there are important consequences. Paediatric specialists are increasingly concerned about the decline of physical activity and sedentary behaviour in young children. A recent study of 8,400 seven-year-olds, carried out by Glasgow University and soon to be published by the *British Medical Journal*, suggests that 3-year old children who watch television for more than 8 hours a week, are at risk of being obese by the age of 7 and of remaining fat for the rest of their lives (See also; Reilly, J. *et al*, 2003a, Reilly, J. *et al*, 2003b).

Christakis *et al* (2004) investigated the effects of television viewing on 1,278 children at age 1 and at age 3. Ten per cent of the sample children were found to have attention problems at age 7 and on average the children were found to be watching an average of 2.2 hours of television per day at age 1, and 3.6 hours at age 3. The study found that efforts to limit television viewing in early childhood may be justified, since early television exposure was associated with attention problems at age 7 even when controlled for confounding factors. An increase of one standard deviation in the number of hours of television watched at age 1 showed a 28 per cent increase in the probability of attention problems by age 7 (Christakis *et al*, 2004).The time spent watching television during child-hood and adolescence has also been found to be significantly associated with leaving school without qualifications, and negatively associated with attaining a university degree. Hancox *et al*, (2005) found that children who watched television for less than one hour per day were the most likely to obtain post school qualifications, including university degrees.

But this doesn't have to be the way it is and Nurseries committed to achieving educational opportunity and social justice can develop educational partnerships with parents and affect home practices. Kenner *et al* (2004) have described how Bangladeshi grandparents in the East End of London were supplied with laptop computers for them to use with their grandchildren. One of the aims of the initiative was to increase family involvement with computers. The authors describe how the grandparents were encouraged to sit beside their grandchildren and help them maintain concentration to complete a range of ICT activities.

> ...the grandparents showed a growing interest in what was happening on the screen. Their curiosity indicated a potential to develop knowledge

and expertise if they were to have access to software or websites which operated in their own language.

Kenner *et al* (2004) go on to argue that providing the Bangladeshi grand-parents with tutoring and resources in Bengali could enhance both their own learning and that of their grandchildren. But yet again, initiatives of this kind require resources that are not always available. It is important to consider the effects of what has become known as the digital divide.

The digital divide

In terms of the general use of ICTs, 2001 survey findings show that 81 per cent of the UK adult population have used a mobile phone, 64 per cent a personal computer, and that 55 per cent have used the internet (Russell and Stafford, 2002). However, women did so less than men, and those in socio-economic groups D and E, those who lived in more deprived residential areas, and those aged 55 and older also used these tech-nologies less. While 79 per cent of Russell and Stafford's (2002) respon-dents in social groups A and B said they had used the internet, only 31 per cent of respondents in groups D and E had ever done so. Just over half of all the adults were found to have a computer at home but this varied from 77 per cent of the socio-economic group A and B respon-dents to just 26 per cent of the D and E respondents. Only 20 per cent of people of D and E social grades had access to the internet at home, com-pared to 43 per cent of the overall population.

According to the Russell and Stafford (2002) survey, most respondents felt that computer skills were important for their future job prospects. There was also a high level of agreement among parents that computer skills were essential to their children's work right now (76 per cent), and would be even more so in the future (98 per cent). In fact a significant factor in determining the use of ICT by adults at present is the presence of children under 16 in their household. The only exception to this is single parent households, where ICT use is generally as low as in house-holds without children. For the 14 per cent of adults who are not using computers but are interested in using them, cost poses a significant barrier. But as 6 and Jupp (2001) suggest, this is probably only a short-term challenge that is largely irrelevant to the underlying issue of exclu-sion and poverty. 6 and Jupp (2001) argue that it is not exclusion from information that matters as much as exclusion by information. Their major concern is the the accumulation of personal information which records individual achievement, merit, risk and entitlement:

We have always lived in information economies. What is really new is that we are now in a personal information economy – one that produces, manipulates, stores and trades personal data on a global industrial scale. Personal profiles are now the basic fuel on which the economy runs. This means that the debate about information exclusion should really focus on the extent to which we want untrammelled meritocracy. This, too, is a debate which has been focused on the wrong issue. Traditionally, it has been understood as being about whether organisations promoted or re-warded those who are brightest , whether they should and whether the brightest form a closed caste. But intelligence is like any other charac-teristic on which people are classified, sorted and judged. It is only as meaningful as the instruments by which we measure it and only as fixed in its determination of people's fate as the institutions that manage its classification. (6 and Jupp, 2001)

Thirty one per cent of all the adults who do not use computers are not interested in doing so. This disinterest in computers is higher among older age groups, with 86 per cent of non-users aged 55 or above not interested, but it also includes 31 per cent of the 16 to 34 year old non-users:

Just over half of all non-users say that there are no incentives to make use of computers... and the internet. This is higher among people aged 55 or more. (Russell and Stafford, 2002)

As Steyaert (2002) has suggested, the extent to which the so-called digital divide matters to the individual will depend in part on the extent to which society continues to support citizens who choose not to be connected or whether such a choice will be made problematic – as is now the case in, for instance, choosing not to have a bank account. But in understanding why it is that so many are disinterested, we should also consider the kind of information that is made available through the internet. Steyaert (2002) cites Childres and Post's (1975) US '*sample of information needs of citizens in lower socio-economic groups:*

■ *Where is the most accessible and cheap child care in this neighbour-hood*

■ *How can I get rid of the rats in the vacant house next door*

■ *My husband left me, what can I do*

■ *How can I know there is lead in the plumbing or painting of this rental flat*

■ *Where do I get some money to buy us food up to the next pay-cheque?*

Steyaert (2002) points out that these information needs are not addressed on the internet. We need to question why not, and to ask why information is seldom provided in community languages. It is clear that giving more access to the internet will not provide greater access to information of this kind. We need to recognise, Steyaert suggests, that the digital divide does not create new fault lines in society but replicates the existing social stratification.

As the DTI, Steyaert (2002) and Warschauer (2003) have all argued, a rethink of the digital divide is essential. The DTI report (2000) presents the findings of Policy Action Team 15 (PAT 15) on the use of ICTs to tackle social exclusion. Their remit was provided by the Social Exclusion Unit's (SEU) 1998 report and the PAT 15 members, and members of the working groups were drawn from relevant policy divisions in Whitehall departments and government offices. The DTI stated that:

> Our central argument is that the debate has been misconceived, because it has focused on the wrong issue. Access to the hardware that gets people online has, up to now, occupied most attention. But the real price of access to kit is falling, and a wider set of issues about content, skills, uses and the wider social consequences are becoming much more important. In the longer run, it is exclusion by information which matters most, rather than exclusion from information. The rise of an economy fuelled by detailed personal profiles creates the risk that, if those profiles are handled and interpreted rigidly, many people could be excluded from basic services and opportunities essential to achieving a decent standard of living. (DTI, 2000)

PAT15 argued that the problems experienced by black and minority ethnic groups were the same as those of everyone living in deprived neighbourhoods: poverty, unemployment, poor educational achievement, crime etc. But they also argued that these were exacerbated by 'racial prejudice and violence, poor perceptions of black and minority ethnic groups, inadequate recognition of the complexity of black and minority ethnic groups and language barriers' (DTI, 2000).

PAT 15 argued that ICT should not be seen or presented as an end in itself but as a means to an end. For activities to engage people more effectively, they should be focused not *on* ICT but *by* it. To illustrate:

> At the *New Start Project* in Cardiff, a group of older Muslim women took sewing classes. One afternoon a computer happened to be on a desk in a corner of the room and they tried it out during their break. They found that they could access patterns through the internet. Interest through this

was generated and three of the women have now developed a network of over 300 women and children. There was no focus on technology, the interest was sparked by chance. This has led them to exploring other activities such as E-mail and self-publishing. (DTI, 2000)

As the report goes on to argue, the central aim should not be to increase uptake and access to ICTs so much as to use them as a tool for community development. The same argument can equally be applied to the educational context. If we are to encourage parents to use ICT with their children at home we should do more to support them in using technology for their own purposes, to satisfy their own needs. One way of achieving that is by providing better online support for their children.

The digital divide cannot be blamed for inequality in education; it has been around for far longer than ICT and is part of a much wider problem. As the Pisa exercise has shown, privileged students do better in the UK, but this is not inevitable. Inequality is much greater in the UK than in Japan. As suggested in Chapter 3, this is the great challenge of personalisation and ICT could make a significant contribution.

Implications for global inequality

According to Steyaert and Gould (2004), London has more internet addresses (urls) than the whole of Africa. With the population of Africa about 800 million, and London's about 7.5 million, that means London currently has over 100 times the number of websites per head of population. What are the prospects for this to change?

The innovative use of NetMeeting in collaborative drawing in some of the rural Allentejo (Portuguese) nurseries involved in the Datec project was mentioned in Chapter 2. Once when we visited one of these nurseries a 4 or 5 year old offered us a picture she had drawn on the computer. At the time we unthinkingly declined the offer and asked the practitioner to explain to the child that we didn't wish to take the picture because we thought it was so good, that she should take it home and show it to her parents. The child was clearly amused and went straight back to the computer and printed another copy to show us how easy it was to solve the problem. Her confidence and capability with the technology impressed us so we asked the practitioner whether this girl had a computer at home. She took us to the window, pointed to a small, and rather dilapidated cottage, and told us that not only did she have no computer at home, she had no electricity. It is hard to imagine what impact ICT may have on the life of this child, but there can be no doubt that it has the possibility of empowerment.

Figure 6 : Equality and reading literacy

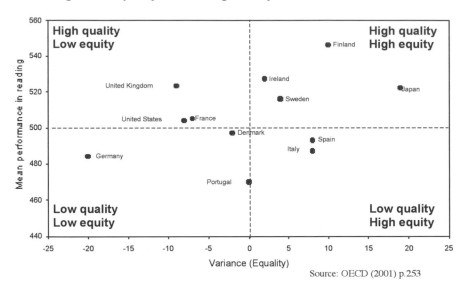

Source: OECD (2001) p.253

Figure 6: Equality and reading literacy

In 2001 we visited the headquarters of NIIT LTD, an ICT training company in New Delhi, to see 'the hole in the wall experiment' (Image 27). The experiment was set up by Sugata Mitra, the head of research at NIIT. The project required having a computer with a high-speed internet connection to be embedded in the concrete wall of the factory that overlooked an urban slum. Community representatives were told the facility was provided for them but were given no instructions on how to use it. The result was that children from the shanty town, mostly 4 to 12 year olds, illiterate and with little or no knowledge of English, quickly taught themselves how to browse the internet. They discovered games they could play on Disney.com and they taught themselves how to use the MS Paint programme provided. A few days after this, they were briefly shown that the computer was capable of playing music files and had soon downloaded free MP3 players, discovered a Hindi music site and were playing their favourite songs.

Image 27

They invent their own terminology for what's going on. For example, they call the pointer of the mouse sui, which is Hindi for needle. More interesting is the hourglass that appears when something is happening. Most Indians have never heard of an hourglass. I asked them, 'What does that mean?' They said, 'It's a damru,' which is Hindi for Shiva's drum. [The God] Shiva holds an hourglass – shaped drum in his hand that you can shake from side to side. So they said the sui became a damru when the 'thing' [the computer] was doing something. (Mitra cited by Judge, 2000)

These findings were duplicated in 30 locations across India and in Cambodia (see http://www.hole-in-the-wall.com/index.html). Apart from justifying the provision of public access information kiosks, they demonstrate the fact that modern ICTs are already intuitive. As computers become cheaper, they also become more user friendly all the time. A great deal can be achieved with minimal instruction if the information acquired is considered useful, interesting or enjoyable. Few educational users now expect to have to read instructions before they can operate a new application. For early educators who are concerned to contribute towards social justice, a significant challenge may be to provide more educational, relevant and bilingual resources on the internet.

As McNulty (2003) has argued, the internet can help establish social justice through:

Democracy – providing alternative news, facilitating communication and making information available.

Equality – the nature of digital intellectual property is such that it can be easily shared.

Autonomy – providing anonymity for those who experience discrimination.

The use of the internet for fraud and to distribute pornography continue to be problems but they are problems which pre-date the internet, and are open to solution through the traditional agencies of law. Language also provides a significant barrier on the internet so it is important to provide multilingual resources. But technology is developing rapidly to provide solutions to these problems. Speech processing applications are being developed to convert speech into text and speech synthesis converts text into speech. 'Machine translation' applications can translate one language into another (see http://babelfish.altavista.com/ and http://www.google.co.uk/language_tools?hl=en). None of these technologies have yet been perfected but significant progress is already being made. As Behar and Silberman (2000) declared:

A Net that doesn't speak English as its default language is coming soon, and machine translation will be one of the best ways to deal with multilingual overload – if we can make it work.

5

ICT Training, Policy Development and Planning

The work we carried out in support of the IBM KidSmart initiative in Europe is described in Chapter 8, but the aspect of that work which has wider relevance is described here. In May 2003 IBM convened a European Conference in Brussels on *Early Learning in the Knowledge Society*. The programme was strongly informed by our work with pre-schools associated with the DATEC project, and our early evaluations of the progress being made in the KidSmart programme in Europe. This provided the principle focus for discussions about the wider implications of ICT in early childhood. The delegates, drawn from 21 countries, felt that knowledge building and co-operation was required at regional, national and European levels to help disseminate research findings, share best practice, and assist policy development for Early Learning (IBM, 2003). The conference made four significant policy recommendations:

> **To include Early Learning in national ICT strategies for education**: National policy strategies for the use of ICT in education should provide a strong ICT component that is well embedded into educational goals and strategies for early childhood education. They should ensure proper continuity of provision and support as children make the transition from Early Learning settings to primary school. For example, this should allow the transfer and continuation of work on such things as 'digital portfolios.' As part of the national strategy, a broad definition of ICT should be adopted (to include computers and a wide variety of other devices and applications). ICT needs to be understood as a multifunctional tool for Early Learning that is used to introduce and support real life ex-

periences and physical activities but not to replace them. Based on existing best practice and an expanded programme of action research in this area, policy development should focus on the appropriate use of new technologies aligned with pedagogical models which reflect the fact that play, creativity and collaboration remain central to the educational experience of young children. (IBM, 2003)

To provide initial training and ongoing professional development for all practitioners: Policy strategies need to reflect the fact that initial practitioner training and accredited, ongoing professional development is a vital and urgent requirement for the successful implementation of ICT in Early Learning settings. As ICT has the potential to impact on almost every aspect of play and learning in Early Learning environments, it is essential that training is extended to all practitioners and that it should address both pedagogy and the curriculum. Training should provide a means by which good practices, including structured activities, are shared more widely and must help practitioners to integrate computers and a wide range of other devices and applications effectively. In order to embed the training in developmentally appropriate pedagogy, innovative practitioners who are experienced in the use of ICT should be directly involved in the training process, and initial training should equip practitioners with the skills needed to work with parents to provide appropriate educational support using ICT in the home. An assessment should be made of the potential that e-Learning can make to the training of Early Learning practitioners based on existing pilots and one or more demonstration projects funded by European Commission research programmes.(*op cit*)

To optimise ICT policies by supporting parental involvement: Policy strategies should recognise that the successful use of ICT in Early Learning will be optimised if parents are made more aware of the potential of ICT and are encouraged to use ICT themselves as a means of becoming more involved in the education of their children. Work with parents should begin by helping them to recognise and build on their own competencies. Policy makers should investigate the extent to which ICT-equipped Early Learning settings can provide a venue for initiatives aimed at improving adult ICT literacy and skills, particularly within multi-agency programmes aimed at bridging the 'digital divide' and promoting social inclusion. *(op cit)*

To support knowledge building and co-operation at all levels for practitioners, policy makers and parents: Knowledge building and co-operation at regional, national and European levels is needed to help disseminate research findings, share best practice, and assist policy development for Early Learning. Benchmarking of ICT provision in Early

Learning settings in EU Member States should be included in the next phase of the European Commission's e-Learning Programme 2002-2004. Support should also be provided at both a national and European level to develop web portals that will encourage the sharing of experience and knowledge (including that related to children with special needs) and which provide both practitioners and parents with mechanisms for identifying resources that have been evaluated as being suitable for the early years. A clear need for further research into early learning processes and the role of ICT has been identified, and this could be a further action for specific action research networks of Early Learning practitioners and experts. (*op cit*)

Issues of transition and assessment have already been discussed. So has the importance of applying broad definitions to ICT, emphasising play, creativity, collaboration, and parent involvement. This chapter outlines an approach to supporting curriculum development that we have been applying in several national and international contexts. It combines two of the above recommendations, involving practitioners in collaborative and co-operative knowledge building as an integral element of an action research approach to training. But first we need to review what we know about the training needs of early childhood practitioners in the UK. In this we are extremely fortunate in having up-to-date research from the REPEY study and the Kinderet research project.

The Research in Effective Pedagogy in the Early Years (REPEY) project

The DfES funded REPEY project (Siraj-Blatchford *et al*, 2002) involved twelve pre-schools selected for having good to excellent child outcomes on cognitive and social and behavioural development. These settings were effective 'outliers' from 141 settings as part of the Effective Provision of Preschool Education (EPPE) project, which has followed the progress of 3,000+ children since 2000. The children in all twelve REPEY settings were 3-5 years old. Two reception classes were also added to this study. The analysis included child and adult observations (over 400 hours), practitioner and parent interviews and documentary analysis of all policy and other documents. A full account of the REPEY findings is available on the DfES website[1]; our concern here is to report only on those aspects relevant to ICT.

Although the EPPE project findings showed that the twelve centres were all effective in promoting learning, they were found to be less effective in integrating ICT into the curriculum. The 'excellent' strategies they had developed in supporting the children in terms of cognitive and social development tended not to be applied in the context of ICT.

The quality of the ICT learning environment in the settings was measured using an ICT Early Childhood Environmental Rating Sub-scale (ICT-ECERS) (See Appendix C) which has 3 items and covers provisions for the development of:

- information handling and Communication Skills

- access and control of ICT tools

- learning about the uses of ICT

This rating subscale was modelled on the ECERS (Early Childhood Environmental Rating Scale) (Harms, Clifford and Cryer, 1998) and its construction was strongly informed by the English Curriculum Guidance for the Foundation Stage (QCA, 2000). The instrument was originally devised as part of the Developmentally Appropriate Technology in Early Childhood (DATEC) project already mentioned.

The scores attributed to the three items in the subscale reflects the practices observed rather than any future plans the centres might have, but the practitioners were questioned at the end of the observation period for clarification of their current practices.

The ICT-ECERS subscale measures each of the 3 items mentioned above, from 1 to 7 with 1 = inadequate practice, 3 = minimal practice, 5 = good practice and 7 = excellent practice. The following table shows the average level of provision in developing the ICT curriculum in these 'effective' pre-schools according to the ECERS ICT subscale during 2000:

Table 6

ICT ECERS Item:	Item Score:
Information handling and Communication Skills	2.5
Access and control of ICT tools	1.58
Learning about the uses of ICT	2.25

Thus most of the practice observed scored between inadequate and minimal. All but one of the case study settings was equipped with at least one computer that was available for the children's use every day. In one setting (219) the children whose parents paid an extra fee for ICT were given a half an hour computer session each week. About 50 per cent paid for this service while some were reported to be adamant that they did not want their child to do it. In another setting (413) the computer was temporarily positioned outside the manager's office away from the main teaching area, thus restricting its use.

A good deal of uncertainty was expressed by practitioners about the appropriate use of computers. Specific concerns were expressed about the ergonomics of desktop computer use, and about equality of opportunity. Practitioners were also anxious that the children should move around more and spend as much of their time as possible interacting with others. The respondents were especially concerned about how long children spent at the computer (on several occasions individual children were observed to be playing at the computer for up to 40 minutes at a time):

> It varies, some children would go on the computer every day if you let them and others never go near. We do try to encourage the ones who don't very often to take it on. Often we have to wean children off and watch that they're not spending too much time on it (324 int. teach?)

Most respondents reported that the boys spent more time at the computer. One setting gave a good deal of thought to why this was so.

> I said it's equal but after I thought about it, it is more boys. There are quite a large amount of girls who just won't choose to go on. Not because the boys use it more it's just that they don't choose to or want to. (017 int. NN)

While none of the practitioners made any mention of the importance of providing positive role models, in at least one of the settings (421) the children frequently saw a volunteer mother entering book returns at a computer. The solution adopted by many settings has been to introduce some form of rota system to control the children's participation and ensure equal access:

> They're only allowed 10 minutes on the computer, and, if you have a very able capable child on a computer, we allow them 20 or 30 minutes. (306 int. Man2)

> We have a system whereby they get their stickers and then I usually put five or six empty squares on a piece of card so the child puts it's sticker on and then the next one until all five stickers are full. But then you've got the mathematical aspect of 'I'm after so and so' and it's a way of self-monitoring who's going to be on next. Then they can perhaps wander round and do something else until it's their turn they don't just have to sit there.(324 int. teach2)

...the nursery has got a timer a five minute timer. We also put a grid down with everybody's name on it, and told the students to put a smiley face next to their name when they'd had their turn that was when we wanted everybody to have a turn on particular programs, to give them all an opportunity. (421 int. NT)

As Figure 7 shows, children were found to be using the computer mainly as a tool intended to develop creativity (often through computer painting programmes etc), or for the acquisition of literacy.

Figure 7: Curricular areas (proportionally) in which children use computers

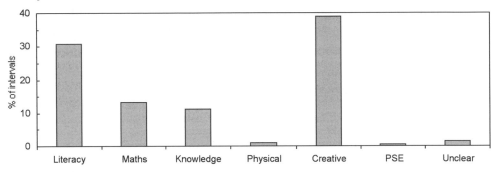

Examining the curricular areas in more detail revealed children experiencing the 'creative' area of the curriculum through computers were split equally between the use of art, music and dance programmes. However, when children used computers for the literacy area they did so almost exclusively through reading (figure 8). The category 'computing hands-on' refers to time the children spent developing general computer skills, for example opening and closing programmes, using the mouse, and printing.

Figure 8: Children's learning activities when computers are used

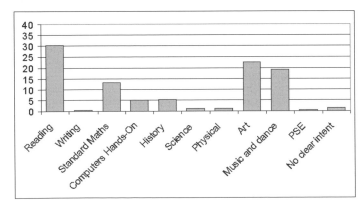

Observation showed frequent examples of practitioners helping children access software and supporting them when they got into difficulties but in only a few cases was this support extended beyond two or three minutes. In most cases adult support was limited to intervention when the children experienced problems or required supervision:

> GIRL 4 (4:2) is at the computer, TEACHER 1 sees she is struggling and kneels down besides her. She explains what to do.
>
> TEACHER 1: 'Keep looking, keep looking. Which one's still moving? Which one's moving? Wait till the square is round the moving one. Press the space bar. Have your hands ready. Quick, press it. Now. Quick. Press it. Wait till it's round that one.'
>
> GIRL 4 (4:2): 'I've done it.'
>
> TEACHER 1: 'Well done' and she returns to her chair.
> (Document '017 obs. 2')

Figure 9 shows which practitioners (if any) were present when the children were computing. The children mostly used computers without an adult. The adults who were present, were likely to be qualified teachers (Level 5).

Figure 9: The adults who engage with children in computing activities

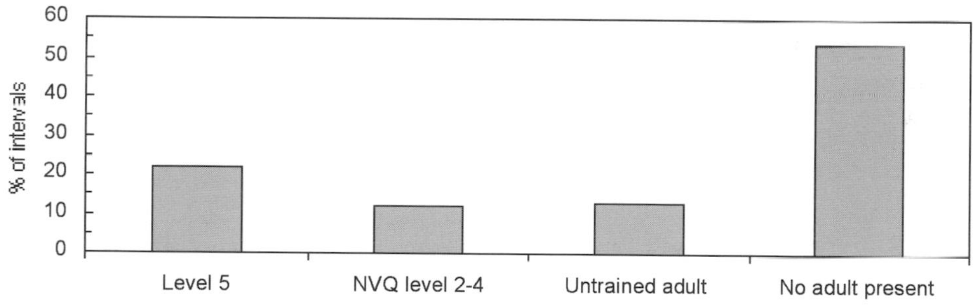

In settings that were accustomed to having an adult working for extended periods with small groups of children, the computer appeared more easily integrated into the curriculum. Without this, difficulties sometimes arose. One practitioner explained the difficulty clearly:

> I suppose that's part of the way that we want to work is to be able to step in and out of their learning. It's more difficult to have things that need to be kept controlled. That involves changing our way of working a little bit. (Document '426 int NT')

Figure 10 displays the proportions of different cognitive pedagogical interactions that practitioners engaged in with children while they were computing. It shows that most practitioners commonly used direct teaching and monitoring interactions with children whilst they were computing.

Figure 10: Cognitive pedagogical interactions

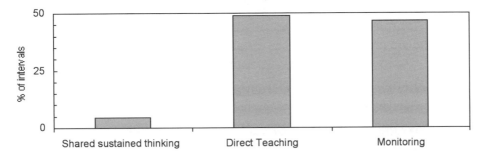

In terms of social pedagogical interactions, two main types of social interaction were employed: encouragement (65 per cent) and behaviour management (35 per cent). As Figure 11 shows, children were generally left to work independently, with the practitioner providing encouragement, questioning, instructing and managing only when required. Interestingly, practitioners rarely engaged in scaffolding and there was little evidence of 'sustained shared thinking' during children's computing activities.

Figure 11: Cognitive pedagogical interaction sub-categories

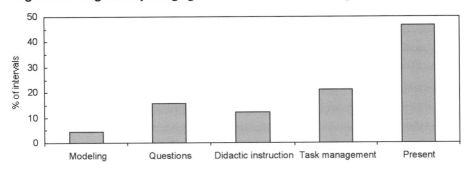

The practitioners were specifically asked what they thought children learned from their time at the computer. Their responses were often defined by the declared objectives of the software being applied but their responses also clearly demonstrated their lack of confidence. In common with many other contemporary studies (e.g. Siraj-Blatchford, J.

and I., 2000a), the most frequent references were made to the development of hand-eye co-ordination and the fine motor skills associated with
controlling the mouse. Several respondents also said it was important for
the children to gain confidence with the technology because they would
be required to use it when they started school. While the value of the
computer in supporting number and language and literacy was mentioned, and many respondents commented on the children's on-screen
painting, few practitioners were using the equipment to achieve specific
learning goals:

> Well I suppose they're learning the basic skills of how a keyboard works
> and how the mouse works. (And there are) number and letter pro-
> grammes that we have so there's the recognition and the counting and
> things like that. But other than that I'm not really sure what they do learn,
> we just like them to be familiar with the keyboard and the mouse and
> generally how it works because we know that computers will be part of
> their school life. (Setting 106 interview NNEB)

> For me their main use is for them to just become familiar with the equip-
> ment and not to be phased by them if they don't have access to them at
> home. So when they move into school they're familiar and comfortable
> with using it and they don't do mindless staring at the screen activities.
> That's really the bottom line. (Setting 214 interview Manager 2)

In only two settings was the potential of the computer in motivating children in terms of emergent early literacy emphasised and the equipment
clearly being exploited effectively to that end:

> ...some children find it a very attractive medium, so that the more formal
> methods of learning, which might not work for some children, work here.
> (Setting 306 interview Manager 2)

In most settings, the children worked at the computer in groups of two to
four and several respondents referred to the quality of the children's
collaboration. However, our observations and at least one respondent
suggested that the quality of interaction was rather variable:

> They learn how to fight at the computer. We don't have much fighting,
> but when we do, it's at the computer. Girls can take or leave the com-
> puter, some of them are quite interested but boys love it. The computer
> is quite good for some of the brighter children, and the ones who have a
> computer at home, and it can stretch them, the ones that are beginning
> to know letters and are really good with their numbers, but I would be
> quite happy not to have a computer in the nursery because it is the most
> unsociable piece of equipment you could wish to imagine. It's extremely

> frustrating.... Very often it's not over a game but a fight over the mouse. (Setting 417 interview Manager)

In one setting we heard how practitioners had discovered an innovative means of extending the children's collaboration by running two adjacent computers with the same software at the same time.

> We've got the two computers so we had 'dressing the teddy' and you hear the conversation 'I've put this sock on' and 'I've put the shoe on' and they're looking at each other and each other's screens and discussing the program. It's interesting to see how they dress it and the sequence they do it in. (Setting 214 interview Ed. worker)

Some respondents also expressed reservations about the use of some aspects of ICT but the general level of provision was closely related to the resources that were available:

> I haven't got them [programmable toys] here. I have used them and I do think that they do have their uses. I find some of those things are quite disruptive from a management point of view because there's an awful 'I want a go, I want a go, I want a go!' as opposed to the actual just looking at what it teaches us and how are we doing it, possession is nine-tenths of it. (Setting 426 interview Teacher)

> ...And we've used an overhead projector a lot this time, so the children can write some stories. And we use a keyboard in the writing area. We've got 10 electronic pianos in the music areas, so they've got keyboards as well. (Setting 421 interview Teacher)

In some settings a good deal of print is displayed and wide use is made of the computer to produce labels and titles in displays, but in others these uses were relatively limited. While many respondents recognised the part cassette recorders, telephones, scanners, and digital cameras (at that time) could play, we found little evidence of settings using programmable toys, and the integration of work on the computer screen with activities off screen was rare. The most innovative work recorded involved digital cameras and scanners.

The potential of integrating ICT within socio-dramatic play was not fully recognised but there were some examples of good practice.

> Well we always have telephones around, sometimes we have an office area (we haven't at the moment – it's being used) so that gets used and we have things like little calculators. But it's for mainly role-play I would say, that they use those. (Setting 106 documentary analysis)

> Yes, they use mobile phones in their play, make-believe ones that they make out of Mobilo or whatever they can find, they make some very good phones actually. They have it flipped and everything and Mobilo is very good for that and they do use that in their play. (Setting 214 interview Ed-worker)

> ...we use telephones that don't work for review times and role-plays. They've got the idea. We have a little TV monitor and a very old video which we'll put perhaps into a house area. Or into a shop so that they can see the prices coming up on the set up. So we do use them in imaginative play. We do use the copier, the cameras. The children can take photographs. The digital cameras they find difficult, and even some of the staff still hold it up to our eyes. (Setting 324 interview teacher)

The benefits of in-service training were clear to respondents and they generally looked forward to finding the time and resources to develop their capabilities further. A particular priority in this for many staff was to gain further knowledge of how to use the technology more effectively specifically with young children.

> I freely admit that ICT is not my strength, I really do need some better training. I'd like to go on a course with somebody who really knew a lot about working with computers with under fives. One of the things I find really frustrating is they break down so much. Somebody I know who's familiar with computers says that's because too many people are using it. If you have one computer with lots of users the computer's going to do funny things. And it's very hard to stop children sticking their fingers in and playing with the keys, it's just so frustrating when they won't work. I'd really like some training by somebody who could inspire me because I'm sure there are lots of lovely ways I could be using ICT for imaginative play. (Setting 214 interview teacher)

The REPEY research findings suggest that even in the case of the effective settings (in terms of the EPPE Cognitive and Social outcomes), the ICT curriculum (in 2001) was at a relatively early stage of development in England. Practitioners remained unclear about the learning objectives and although computers were seen as valuable resources, there was still a great deal to be done to integrate the technology into the pre-school learning environment. Despite these limitations, some degree of innovation was already apparent and examples of effective practice were identified. But it was clear that further training, especially training focused specifically upon the needs of young children, was called for and would be well received.

Training needs and opportunities

The Editors of *New Perspectives for Learning* (pjb Associates, 2003) were cited earlier to draw attention the considerable research evidence that demonstrates that: 'The use of technology in classrooms is found to be socially contextualised, interacting with the institutional and organisational cultures of schools and reflecting elements of the prevailing social relations in and around the context of use'.

This has particularly important implications for training. As Galton (2000) has argued, practitioners value research when it is focused on specific teaching and learning contexts and practices. But few research interventions so far have led to sustained change in partner institutions. Galton cites McLaughlin in arguing that teaching and learning research products therefore need to be anchored in concrete teaching contexts. As Black and William (1998) put it:

> Teachers will not take up attractive sounding ideas, albeit based on extensive research, if these are presented as general principles which leave entirely to them the task of translating them into everyday practice – their classroom lives are too busy and too fragile for this to be possible for all but an outstanding few. What they need is a variety of living examples of implementation, by teachers with whom they can identify and from whom they can both derive conviction and confidence that they can do better, and see concrete examples of what doing better means in practice.

Resources are also required if changes are to be sustained. Teachers need to be aware of the overall objectives of the changes, and to be involved in extended 'supportive communities of practice' that include the senior managers.

The European KINDERET project funded by the EU (Leonardo da Vinci) adopted this model. The project aimed to identify and understand the theoretical and practical needs of early childhood educators in terms of their use of ICT and to work in collaboration with them in developing resources to support their colleagues.

The Kinderet survey was applied in 2004 to identify practitioner training needs[2]. The six page questionnaire was composed of eighteen questions roughly divided into four subsections to elicit the following information:

- the personal and professional characteristics of respondents
- how ICT was applied to the curriculum
- the availability and application of ICT resources
- the training needs and preferences of practitioners

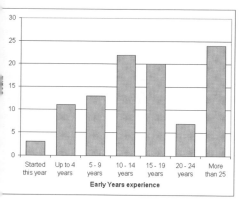

Figure 12

The survey was carried out with an opportunity sample provided through their involvement in the IBM KidSmart initiative. A characteristic common to the settings was that they had been selected for involvement with IBMs KidSmart programme because they were serving the needs of relatively disadvantaged communities. All the settings involved would have at least one computer and many have benefited from training provided as a condition of their LEA's involvement in the initiative. A total of 99 valid questionnaires were returned.

The questionnaires represent the views of an eclectic range of practitioners from a variety of pre-school settings and with a range professional qualifications (34.34 per cent Graduate, 40.40 per cent Further Education and 25.25 per cent 'Other'). In terms of the respondents' years of experience (see Figure 12), the largest proportion fell between 10-19 years with many having 25+ years experience.

While it might have been assumed that years of experience and the age of the respondents would have been a good predictor of varying opinions of the value of Information and Communication Technology, this does not seem to be the case. No significant correlation was found between the age of respondent and length of service and their confidence in or concerns for ICT. Although 91.9 per cent of respondents believed ICT was an 'important' or 'very important' area of the curriculum, only 38 per cent felt that they had been given sufficient training to provide it. Individual respondents who were less motivated might have indicated that the technology was being used inappropriately. One respondent, for example, reported: 'I do feel it [the computer] has a detrimental effect on speaking and listening skills – less interaction with peers, staff etc' (R 57). This suggests that either inappropriate 'drill and practice' or – worse – 'arcade' games were being mainly used.

Figure 13 shows the particular areas of the curriculum to which practitioners felt ICT could most contribute. The respondents were asked what objectives they had for the use of ICT and were asked separately what they felt that children learned from their use of the tools. Interestingly, their responses were quite different. While only 5 per cent reported specific software skills (e.g. number/letter recognition etc) as an

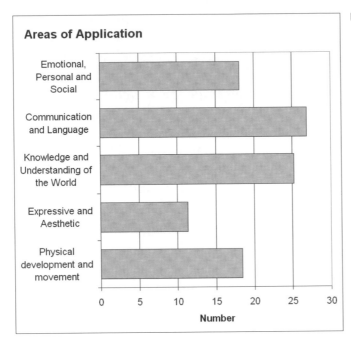

Figure 13

Areas of Application

Number

educational objective of using ICT, 20 per cent felt this was a major learning outcome.

Similarly, only 3 per cent considered the development of social skills (e.g. sharing/turn taking) as a learning objective, and 23 per cent saw it as a learning outcome. The references to social skills referred exclusively to issues of co-operation, which suggests the need to raise practitioners' awareness of the importance of children talking together and developing their collaboration skills. It is also significant that while the development of fine motor skills such as mouse control was seen as an important objective and outcome (25 per cent and 23 per cent respectively), the development of technological awareness/technology education through using ICT was considered important as an objective by only 16 per cent, and observed as a learning outcome by a mere 6 per cent. Again this suggests the need to raise awareness of the issues. It seems likely that the reduced proportion of practitioners emphasising fine motor skills as an important learning outcome, compared with the REPEY and earlier Kid-smart findings, was a reflection of the training provided through the Kid-Smart initiative.

Table 7 shows the responses to the question about the criteria used to select computer software. Interestingly, only two respondents referred to the children's own opinions in this and only one mentioned the need to

Table 7: Software Selection Criteria

Category	Number of respondents who rated this important
Age appropriate	44
Developmental Appropriate	22
Educational	34
Graphics/Visual/Audio	26
Child Friendly/Ease of Use	39
Fun/Interesting	18
Recommendation	6
Price/Cost	9

avoid software depicting violence. In fact all the responses were highly generalised and provide little information about what criteria the practitioners might apply in judging the software 'appropriate' or 'educational'.

Practitioners are concerned about the difficulties inherent in evaluating ICT applications prior to purchase and many are actively seeking support with this.

As the QCA (2004) recently reported, in the Foundation Stage we are still in a situation where: '*many practitioners are not confident enough with their own use of ICT to allow children to use technology to enhance their learning in all areas*' (p7).

The analysis of the practitioners' wishes about training courses is provided in table 2, and shows few surprises. In the practical delivery of training, number seven on the list of priorities, the need for training on 'software evaluation', might usefully be collapsed into number two; 'working with recommended software'. The emphasis on desktop publishing and the creation of web pages reflects the desire among many practitioners to create their own resources and to present the children's work more effectively to parents. The explicit reference to programmable toys in the Desirable Learning Outcomes has led to their widespread introduction but training has failed to keep up with provision in this area.

While a number of reports refer to practitioners having fairly high levels of access to the internet and to e-mail, they are scarcely used in the foundation stage. According to the evaluators of Evaluation of Curriculum Online (Finch and Kitchen, 2004), only 10 per cent of teachers in nursery schools and 15 per cent in primary schools reported use of internet resources with the children once a week or more often.

The study also showed that 19 per cent of nursery schools and 11 per cent of foundation stage classes in primary schools still have no internet connection for the children to use. As the sample for this study did not include private and voluntary sector providers, this may seriously understate the problem. It is likely that questions related to simple access to the internet leave many of the realities of the situation hidden. The DfES (2003) Survey of Information and Communications Technology in Schools didn't collect statistics for the foundation stage, but it has reported, for example, that only 60 per cent of all primary school teachers have e-mail accounts provided and funded by their school, LEA, BECTA or the DfES. The percentage of foundation stage practitioners without such access will almost certainly be much greater.

The poor reliability and the inadequate support so often offered in maintaining ICT equipment has been a recurring complaint. So the desire expressed to learn more about computer maintenance and computer troubleshooting is not surprising. The wishes expressed by practitioners to learn more about curriculum integration and about the nature, aims and objectives of computer and technology education is particularly encouraging, given the arguments presented above. These areas do appear to be priorities for development.

The Kinderet respondents were also asked about the reasons they had not attended ICT courses in the past. Lack of time was cited by 54 per cent of respondents as the main reason. Lack of financial support was another frequently cited reason (46 per cent). The lack of time may also indicate an awareness of the financial implications for their employer, as

Table 8: Training required

	Training Areas	per cent of answers
1	Office Tools (e.g. PowerPoint)	70,0
2	Working with new (recommended) software	67,3
3	Desktop publishing (e.g. Publisher – text handling, graphics and images)	59,6
4	Programmable toys, floor and screen turtles	56,4
5	How to create web pages	55.8
6	ICT Curriculum Integration	53.1
7	Evaluating educational software	52.9
8	Computer maintenance and troubleshooting	51.9
9	Computer/Technology education	46.5
10	Training to use e-mail	44.7

most training courses are offered during the school day, which would require the setting to factor in the cost of supply cover or put aside an in-service day for training, when there are many items competing for attention. Kinderet also enquired about the respondents' preferred timing of training.

Little interest was expressed in the options of 'evening in-service' and 'supported self-taught' courses. This may suggest a problem with training outside of school hours, as both evening and self-taught courses require practitioners to use their own time. However, both the whole-day and half-day in-service options allow practitioners to access the training they need during regular working hours, while being paid regular working wages.

Practical workshops were the most favoured form of training (73 per cent), with single short subject courses the second most popular, though only 31 per cent of respondents preferred this. Training opportunities that involve self-directed learning (distance learning, on-line training) and/or those that seem to have a more theoretical basis (discussion seminars, accredited certified training courses) attracted little interest. It appears that most practitioner respondents – who cited insufficient time as one of the main reasons for not attending training sessions – want to be provided with practical suggestions based on the trainers' own practical experience, which they can then apply in their own classrooms. When asked about appropriate institutions or authorities to provide ICT training, the respondents chose local schools and the local authority as the most suitable. Universities and hardware and software manufacturers were both regarded as inappropriate. While universities and industrial companies may be both proficient and resourced to offer ICT training, they may appear less suitable to early years practitioners who want training to be practical and relevant to day-to-day application. Accordingly, local schools and local authority organisations who have access and knowledge of the relevant foundation stage curriculum and associated expectations seem the 'safer' and more suitable choice.

Many practitioners continue to feel insecure about their use of technology in the classroom and it was argued at an early stage in the development of the Kinderet project that training should take two dimensions into account: the attitudes of practitioners and the acquisition and development of knowledge, understanding and skills. But as Carioca (1997) argued, in the processes of practitioner training, we must also recognise the need to develop positive dispositions towards life-long learning: '... *teachers' personal and professional development must be faced as a subsystem of a lasting education process*' (*op cit* p139).

Carioca *et al* (2005) cites Blázquez's (1996) 'essential postulates' of training in arguing for a training model that includes each of the following assumptions:

- that initial training and lasting/continuous training should be a *continuum*
- that a training plan must be based on the inclusion of theory and practice
- that research-action must be faced by teachers as a kind of; 'theory of making conceptual the practical field, the effective practices of professional daily life'
- that training plans must focus essentially on teachers' real problems and needs
- that training should be based on a diagnosis of specific needs, so as to acquire and deepen the professional skills
- that cooperative work should be valued
- that training respect the isomorphism of principles and practices, which implies choosing the modalities which make it easy to fulfil this principle, including the conquest of autonomy, sharing the 'power' of assessing the training process.

Each of these principles has been applied in developing our approach to training, which has typically developed according to the following stages:

1. The collaborative identification of needs and opportunities
2. The provision of ICT specific training and resources
3. Supporting practitioners in the collection of evaluative evidence
4. Providing the infrastructural resources that are required to allow practitioners to continue sharing their work beyond the immediate period of engagement

In the following chapters we provide three case studies that illustrate this approach further. The first is an example at the centre level, reporting on the work carried out with the Gamesley Early Excellence Centre in Glossop in Derbyshire. The second involved work at a regional level, and we report on our collaboration with Northamptonshire local education authority. And the third reports on work carried out at national and international level with IBM and their KidSmart initiative.

Notes

1 http://www.dfes.gov.uk/research/data/uploadfiles/RB356.pdf

2 For further details of the project see: http://www.eseb.ipbeja.pt/kinderet/

6

Case Study 1
Gamesley Early Excellence Centre

amesley Early Excellence Centre (EEC) is acknowledged as a
leading centre of exemplary practice in education and care for
children and families in the UK. They are inundated with visitors,
who come from all over the world to observe and learn from their practice. They have worked to establish an excellent reputation across the
curriculum, providing sound assessment procedures for young children
with emphasis on continuity and progression in learning, leading under
3s provision and some inspiring provision for special educational needs
(SEN). This case study describes their contribution, and shows how this
was achieved in just one of these areas: ICT.

Our work with Gamesley began in 2000, when the ICT curriculum was at
an early stage of development. The staff were extremely well motivated
from the start and individual members of staff had already developed
significant ICT strengths. They were, for instance, already making their
own *My World* (Dial Solutions) screens to support a range of curriculum
applications. Our work with the setting was supported by their involvement in both the DATEC and IBM Kidsmart projects, and the initiative
was developed further by the Centre. Gamesley has thus continued to
influence the practice of many other settings.

In January 2003 the ICT co-ordinators, Cathy Jones and Carole Bennett
received a BECTA Award (British Education and Communications Technology Agency) for *Innovation and Change* in the field of information
and communications technology (ICT). This was the first national ICT
award to be presented to a pre-school setting in the UK. The training

team have subsequently won a BECTA second award in 2005 for advice and support in ICT. The Centre has also gained a NAACE quality mark in ICT in the Early Years.

Context of the Centre

Gamesley Early Excellence Centre (DfES 'early excellence' status achieved 1999) is a purpose built, integrated nursery centre providing early years education, family support, adult education and training for other early years providers in the private, voluntary and maintained sectors. It originally opened in 1973. It is maintained and supported by the education and social services departments of Derbyshire County Council and has a large multidisciplinary staff. It has recently become a Children's Centre under a Government initiative as part of the new children's agenda. The centre has flexible opening hours from 7.30am – 6.00pm and it is open all year round. It is set in a disadvantaged area and up to 40 per cent of children enter the nursery with delayed language.

The provision for children includes a nursery for 0-5 year olds, an out of school club for children aged 4-11 years and a crèche. There are toy libraries, book libraries and a listening library. Adults can also access education and training at the centre. ICT classes providing accredited courses take place in an eight place computer suite. All courses are free and are open to adults such as teachers, tutors, and nursery nurses. Other classes deal with family support and education, parenting classes. Gamesley provides ICT links with the employment services through a stand alone touch screen computer situated in the entrance hall.

As an EEC and Children's Centre, Gamesley is also funded to provide extensive in-house and outreach training and support for early years practitioners, especially the local private and voluntary sector. Increasingly, workshops, seminars and courses on ICT in the Foundation stage are provided both locally and nationally.

An Acorn computer was installed in the centre in 1995. For many staff, this was their first experience of a computer and some were afraid to use it in case they broke or damaged it. The whole staff spent an inservice day at an ICT centre at Matlock learning about their computer, after which some used it for making labels for coat pegs or for writing up their child observations. They enjoyed desktop publishing and produced letters, booklets, posters etc. Although most of her skills were self taught, Cathy Jones, already an accomplished artist, attended courses for desk top publishing and to learn a programme called 'Draw'. She then created MY World screens for use across the setting on the three Acorn computers bought by the centre.

In 1996 the setting was selected to take part in evaluating a Casio digital camera, a scheme run by the Derbyshire Education Support Centre for ICT (DESCIT). The staff were impressed with the camera and found a multitude of applications for it. They took it on trips, made games for the children with it, and helped them to take and print their own photographs. The teachers at the centre received New Opportunities Fund (NOF) training and some Family Support Workers attended computer courses run by DESCIT. In 1999 a home PC was purchased for use in the nursery and this proved to be something of a turning point. The PC was preferred because it was just like the computers some of the staff had at home. Their confidence quickly grew.

In 1999, still only a handful of staff at the Centre were interested in ICT, and labels for coat pegs were about the limit of their efforts. Now, every member of the nursery staff has developed skills on the PC for their personal use or to use it with the children:

> At first there were probably three or four of us that were keen, now every single person uses it at some point of the week. Whether it's for doing records or looking for information. Everyone uses it. There are a couple that aren't as keen but they still use it. I'd say 98 per cent of them. (Cathy Jones and Carole Bennett)

Almost everyone is now comfortable using computer technology and most can take and print photographs with a digital camera, which are then presented in the children's records or in displays around the nursery or to make games for the children to use at home. Most staff now use the scanner to reproduce the children's work such as drawings or collage:

> I feel that in the last twelve months the staff have come on leaps and bounds. They are using all the equipment now and of course the children should come first but [the staff] have got to learn ways of doing things. They are getting there. They are using the scanner to scan in children's work to put in the records and I think they'll be able to do more. (Cathy Jones and Carole Bennett)

More than half the staff use the internet to send e-mails or to find information. A few use the digital video camera to record outings and events in the nursery or to observe children at play. It has been used to record the Christmas Concert, played back via the TV for the children to watch and recorded to VHS videotape and sold to raise funds for Centre. All staff use some form of technology to promote ICT with the children each day, in line with their planned weekly and termly programme. Two teachers have received on line training from *Capita Learning and Development* and two of the family support workers have completed the European Computer Driving Licence (ECDL) course. Several other staff have completed the Computer Literacy and Information Technology (CLAIT) course.

In-house training and development

Our first input to the Centre was in 2000 when ICT training was provided for the whole staff. ICT was presented from the start as much more than desk-top computers. ICT was presented as one part of a broader 'Technology Curriculum', and the staff were introduced to contemporary debate about the nature of technological literacy. ICTs were identified as providing a range of sophisticated tools to support communication and control.

At that stage the Gamesley staff had already gained some experience of applying the Early Childhood Environment Rating Scale: Revised (ECERS-R)(Harms *et al*, 1998) and the EPPE project's English extension (ECERS-E) (Sylva *et al*, 2004) as self-assessment measures to improve practice. The word 'environment' in these rating scales is taken in its broadest sense to include social interactions, pedagogical strategies and relationships between children and between adults and children. The scales have been shown to have predictive validity through the results of child outcome measures applied to the 'graduates' of higher or lower rated pre-school environments. Further details of how these tools may be applied as self assessment and improvement instruments at the centre level appear in Sylva *et al* (2003), which identifies these basic requirements:

- Rigorous training should be provided on both the quality criteria and on the use and role of the scales

- The setting must have a critical mass of reflective practitioners

- A 'critical friend' is required to support the initiative (e.g. from the Local Authority or from Higher Education)

- Settings must show a willingness to undergo external validation (i.e. a 'blind assessment carried out by a trained and reliable assessor).

The ECERS rating scales are made up of a number of sub-scales which provide an overview of the pre-school environment and cover aspects of the setting from the furnishing to adult-child interaction and the areas of mathematics, science, literacy and diversity. Each sub-scale is comprised of a range of items describing 'quality' rated from 1 to 7, with 1 = inadequate practice, 3 = minimal practice 5 = good practice and 7 = excellent practice. The observations always start with rating the level 1 practices and each item is worked though systematically. The scores attributed to each of the scales reflect the practices that are observed rather than the future plans of the centre. However, the staff are questioned at the end of the observation period for clarification of their current practices.

A first draft of our ECERS-ICT subscale was introduced and the staff were encouraged to consider where their practice stood on the scale, so as to critically evaluate the items and suggest changes to improve the scale. From this initial audit of current practice the staff were invited to identify the challenges of ICT and to select, from the ICT statements that had not been achieved, both short term and long term curriculum development goals. Appendix C provides a copy of the subscale in its final form (following further trials and consultations).

The ICT ECERS style sub-scale covers provisions for the development of:

- Information handling and Communication Skills
- Access and Control of ICTs tools
- Learning about the uses of ICTs

Discriminant validity for the ICT sub-scale has been based on the ability of the items to distinguish between classrooms of varying quality which have been assessed by independent trainers/experts. It is notable that our external validation of Gamesley's ECERS rating confirmed it as the only pre-school we identified as achieving excellent (level 7) practice in all three areas, and the quality of their provision was later confirmed when they were awarded the prestigious BECTA award.

Image 28

In the early training, the Gamesley staff were also introduced to the DATEC project and given the opportunity to practised applying the DATEC criteria for evaluating ICT applications. Subsequent visits to the Centre were largely focused on evaluating and trialling new applications. One of these was the Sony Mavica digital camera (pictured). As soon as the staff saw the advantages of being able to share the cameras while keeping their own floppy disc file of pictures they ordered four of them:

> We use them all the time. We're always charging batteries up...When you take a picture with any other camera the children say 'let me have a look at it now'. If it's a camera with film they're so disappointed that they can't see it instantly. In under three's they're so used to digital cameras that if I was taking a picture lots of children come to look at the screen. (Cathy Jones and Carole Bennett)

The settings resources now include an improvised close circuit TV system, metal detectors for outdoor play and a wide range of pretend and real ICT props used in socio-dramatic play. But although a vast range of ICT hardware and software is now employed, the approach at Gamesley is not motivated by blind enthusiasm. Every application is critically evaluated:

> We have to remember that active doing is more appropriate for the early years than replicating an activity on a computer. An example of this is creating cards which are better made by hand than on the computer. Sometimes early years staff in some settings may use computers for a variety of inappropriate activities simply because it makes the setting appear up to date, modern and impresses parents. (Cathy Jones and Carole Bennett)

Staff keep digital journals to support collaboration and critical reflection, and to inform parents about the progress being made with ICT. Figure 29 shows a typical entry.

Over the years the staff have made a variety of props to represent real household technology such as washing machines made from cardboard boxes. They have also made working lighthouses and lanterns with a batteries and bulbs.

> In the under 3's department the children have access to pretend equipment. They role play using a toy microwave oven and TV in the home corner. There is a till in the shop area made from a cardboard box and the staff have rigged up a simple circuit to make a buzzer work. The children communicate with each other using old mobile phones, and although not really connected they press the

Figure 14

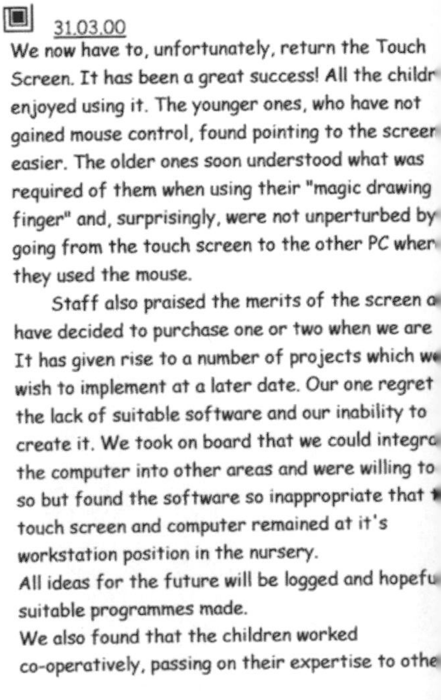

🔲 31.03.00

We now have to, unfortunately, return the Touch Screen. It has been a great success! All the childr enjoyed using it. The younger ones, who have not gained mouse control, found pointing to the screen easier. The older ones soon understood what was required of them when using their "magic drawing finger" and, surprisingly, were not unperturbed by going from the touch screen to the other PC when they used the mouse.

Staff also praised the merits of the screen a have decided to purchase one or two when we are It has given rise to a number of projects which we wish to implement at a later date. Our one regret the lack of suitable software and our inability to create it. We took on board that we could integra the computer into other areas and were willing to so but found the software so inappropriate that t touch screen and computer remained at it's workstation position in the nursery.

All ideas for the future will be logged and hopefu suitable programmes made.

We also found that the children worked co-operatively, passing on their expertise to othe buttons and numbers and have lengthy conversations with each other. (Journal)

We had two year olds twins that absolutely loved the storybook Brown Bear, so I made it into a talking book on the computer and they just absolutely played and played with it and they asked to put it on every day. It wasn't 'on'; they came and asked me, saying 'I want Brown Bear', and I'd put it on for them. (Cathy Jones)

Gamesley has continued to ground their development work on both resource and skills auditing. Hardware includes ICT equipment considered particularly suitable for under 5s such as touch screens, and ICT equipment used to thread throughout the curriculum and support socio-dramatic play. The staff purchase software on approval and send back items they consider unsuitable. They also adapt software to meet the needs of the foundation stage and have developed a range of 'My World' screens, and Junior Multimedia and Junior Multimedia Lab V (Sherston) applications for integrated learning.

Some children aged 3-5 have short concentrations spans and tend to only spend about 4 or 5 minutes on computers. Some will spend a longer period of time because they are working on a piece of work or a game and need time to complete the task. Some who are just learning how to operate the mouse or keyboard, need to be given the opportunity to repeat their new found skills. There are a minority who will spend their entire nursery time on the computer if allowed to do so and will seize every chance to get in front of the monitor. We try to be aware of who these children are and to give them set tasks to challenge them. We work hard to try to ensure that we support all six areas of learning through a wide variety of computer programs. This goes some way to ensuring that children who spend a long time using the computer are actually engaged in purposeful learning tasks which both teach and re-enforce 'The Early Learning Goals' for the half term and which challenge them as individuals. This determination on our part ensures that for children, using the computer rather than more conventional ways can fulfil areas of their learning. We are also aware of children who always work alone on the computers and we try to devise strategies and give opportunities for these children to work together in small groups, in an attempt to develop their collaborative and co-operative skills. The KidSmart bench seat works well in encouraging children to work together, as does the sensitive questioning and intervention by facilitating adults. Every member of staff keeps close records of about ten children whom they know well and have responsibility for assessment. Staff will be aware of their children's developmental needs, whether it be physical, emotional, social, cognitive. It is the focus of staff to steer their children towards activities, which will develop their potential, and away from activities, which are unnecessarily repetitive. (Lynn Kennington)

Images 29, 30 and 31

Examples of applications

The staff at Gamesley often take the children out on visits to learn from their local environment. They learned all about barcoding on one visit to a local supermarket. They saw how the combination of black bars and spaces of varying widths on the barcode attached to each product gives an encoded reference number that the supermarket computer then uses to access a more detailed record of the product price, current stock levels and other descriptive data. They saw how the information from the bar code was scanned into the computer at the checkout using a laser, and how the computer instantly located the item in its database and displayed the price on the cash register. Back at the setting, the staff worked with the children to improvise their own checkout for socio-dramatic play (Image 29). The final version of their improvised bar code scanner included a battery and a buzzer covered with card, which the children pressed as they passed goods over it. Image 30 shows the children using a digital microscope and Image 31 shows a member of staff teaching a child how to use a web cam. Old video recorders, irons and cassette recorders have been provided for the children to dismantle with tools – screwdrivers, spanners etc. – and to see the internal components. Two telephones (not expensive ones) have been set up so the children can speak to each other. Mobile phones/walkie talkies have been made from boxes. Cassette recorders are also widely used, providing a relatively low cost ICT which can be used in a variety of ways in

socio-dramatic play and for re-telling stories, music, dancing, enacting stories etc. Security cameras were purchased and attached to portable TVs to create a closed circuit TV system used for video conferencing. This system, along with a working telephone, encourages interaction, communication and language development. The children love to watch each other play and talk to each other through the cameras. Local shops and supermarkets have donated their old tills and these have been placed in the nursery shop. In the outdoor area, walkie talkies and traffic lights are used, and, at times, objects made of various materials are hidden in the sand play area so that the children can search for them using a metal detector. Old cameras are available for children to 'pretend' play and a video recorder is used to record socio-dramatic play which can be analysed for training, assessment or observation purposes.

Following a visit to a natural history museum, the staff created their own dinosaur museum in the nursery where children could explore and develop their knowledge and understanding of dinosaurs. The children were asked what they would like to see and have in the museum and they said they would like to be able to play with dinosaurs, use the computer, dig for bones, see dinosaurs moving, and 'make it like a real museum!'

A wide range of ICT was used in this integrated curriculum project, including cassette players, videos, karaoke, computer, multi-link tape recorders, all applied to support *Communication, language and literacy*. Programmable toys, an electronic till and computers were used to support the children's *Mathematics*. The digital microscope, metal detector, the internet, digital cameras, pretend barcode scanner, screens, video and television were used to support their *Knowledge and Understanding of the World. Personal, Social and Emotional development* was supported through the use of a multi-link player and cassette recorders, camcorder and digital camera. Using an overhead projector supported the children's *physical*

Images 32 and 33

development and supported their creativity when they used karaoke and paint packages. Further details of this project can be found on the Centre website at: http://www.gamesleyeec.org.uk/parict.asp

Funding sources

The ICT developments have been supported by NOF funding for staff training, a National Grid for Learning (NGfL) grant for hardware, software and cabling etc. The DfES Early Excellence Funding has supported the development of a web site, funded the ICT co-ordinators and their dissemination of good practice, consultancy support, and paid for more hardware and software. Major expenses have included an interactive whiteboard, a digital projector, programmable toys and digital cameras for use by other practitioners in the dissemination and training programme.

In 1999-2000 the Centre successfully applied for a DfES small schools grant of £10,000 to develop their expertise on ICT further and to share their practice with others. This was shared equally with Hadfield Nursery school who worked with them on the project. The funding supported further consultancy support and the purchase of further equipment including a digital camcorder, digital cameras, metal detectors, a scanner, photo-quality printers, programmable toys and web cams.

The Basic Skills Agency literacy and numeracy scheme for parents has involved staff members working with parents on strategies for early reading and number work with children under 5. The Centre was awarded funding to purchase laptops and digital cameras to enable staff and parents to carry out the project.

In 2000, IBM donated two KidSmart computers to the Centre (see Chapter 8), and the Centre's digital microscope was purchased with Tesco supermarket vouchers collected by the parents and staff.

Day to day planning

The Gamesley staff identify specific learning objectives and targets based on the Foundation curriculum guidance and the Early Learning Goals. At weekly team meetings they refine these objectives. Every member of staff plans what they are going to do in the area of the Centre they are working in. ICT is always included in these plans as part of Knowledge and Understanding of the World. A My World screen or a multimedia disc is created to match the chosen story or book for the half term and the staff always try to think of how to incorporate ICT in socio-dramatic play.

Gamesley's first ICT policy was included as a exemplar in the ICT Handbook published by Early Education, *More than Computers* (Siraj-Blatchford, and Siraj-Blatchford, 2000). Progress at Gamesley continues, as their most recent policy statement shows:

Gamesley Early Excellence Centre: ICT Policy
Why do we teach ICT?
We live in a rapidly changing technological world where technologies are extending human capacities. We therefore need to help to prepare pupils to understand, experience and make an active contribution to this world in order to learn, communicate and develop the appropriate skills.

Aims
To encourage children to find out about and identify the uses of technology in their everyday lives and use computers, programmable toys and familiar equipment to support their learning and communication.

To be clear about all learning outcomes as ICT is integrated throughout the Foundation Curriculum

QCA Early Learning Goals
By the end of the reception year most children should be able to: 'Find out about and identify the uses of technology in their everyday lives and use computers and programmed toys to support their learning' (QCA, 2000)

Objectives
- to encourage children to use IT as a tool to access other forms of learning and develop the skills needed to do this

- to develop children's understanding of everyday uses of information and communications technology

- to develop technological literacy through a range of products which children will be familiar with and which will be easily understood and accessed

- to integrate technology in socio-dramatic play as a reflection of the world about us

- to encourage children and staff to use the internet to gain knowledge and support learning

- to use ICT for communication purposes – with parents, other agencies, other early years practitioners and the children and staff with each other

- to encourage children to work collaboratively, sharing knowledge, skills and enjoyment

- to develop a skills-based approach to computer use which puts the child in control of the equipment rather than the other way around

- to integrate ICT throughout the whole of the Foundation Curriculum

- to allow staff to develop professionally through inservice training opportunities.

Teaching and learning approaches

When devising our teaching and learning approaches we will apply the principles of our policy aims and objectives.

* We will use ICT in the delivery of our play-based curriculum and we therefore aim to include a technological application in all the play situations we create. This is because play reflects life experiences for the child which are ICT rich. We will place TVs and videos, working phones, close circuit TVs , computers etc in the shop and home corner so the children are able to access the technology independently, without adult intervention.

- We will have computers in the nursery classroom for children to use independently. We aim for hardware to be child friendly – touch screens, small mice, IBM Kidsmart computers with double seating for collaborative learning and white boards. Our software will be open, child friendly, easily managed and often created by ourselves to meet the needs of the children and tailored to the learning objectives set in the planning.

- We will use our ICT equipment in small group work in order to teach concepts and skills. We will encourage peer group collaboration.

- We will also teach in one to one situations and encourage the use of the headphones at the computer to aid concentration in a busy nursery environment.

Effective and efficient deployment of ICT resources

1. We will use our National Grid for Learning (NGfL) and Early Excellence funding to purchase hardware, network, cabling and e-Learning credits to purchase software. The financial accountability for these budgets remains the head's responsibility and the financial administration the responsibility of the bursar.

2. We will invest in technical support from a reliable provider so our equipment is well maintained and up to date. Currently this is the DCC technical support department.

3. We will invest in internet access of the highest quality so that staff and children have opportunities to access the world wide web to enhance learning.

4. We will also purchase appropriate ICT equipment which is not computer-based for play and to enable children to access the Foundation curriculum.

5. We will aim to provide sufficient computers in the nursery environment for one to twelve children.

6. We will aim to provide appropriate software for children to access computer-based learning independently and aid teaching and learning in the Foundation stage.

7. We will aim to make our learning objectives clear in our planning and measure their effectiveness in assessment and target setting.

8. We will be clear when purchasing resources that the outcomes for the children are based in improving teaching and learning. This will include resources purchased for staff development, parents' use and dissemination of practice.

9. We will aim to provide the head, all teachers, training officer and ICT co-ordinators with laptop computers to aid professional development and to develop resources for the children. Other staff members will be given a laptop computer when finances allow, in order to increase professional development in ICT.

10. Staff will have opportunity to develop professionally through in-house and external training, and funds will be set aside for ICT staff development. Staff will be encouraged to develop their computing skills by using the Life-Long Learning computer suite based at the centre wherever possible.

Planning

Long, medium and short term plans will include ICT. There will also be a cross-curricular, focused approach to planned ICT in the early years curriculum.

Each child has an individual assessment record which is used to inform planning.

Assessment and record keeping

Each child's developmental assessment record will include ICT skills and knowledge which will be continuously used for planning and sharing with parents.

ICT equipment will be used to record the progress of children e.g. their use of the digital camera and computer software.

Equal opportunities and differentiation

All children will have equal access to technological equipment regardless of gender, race, culture or ethnicity, disability or class. However positive action may be taken to ensure that children who have a special need are given priority of access. These needs may be due to physical disability or social need because of financial constraints in the home backgound or to counter any gender bias operating in the boys' and girls' access to technology.

Differentiation within a class group will be implemented through the assessment procedures where each child has an individual education plan, and through the target-setting procedures.

Inclusion, incorporating special educational needs and the gifted and talented

Inclusion benefits all children and helps to promote equal opportunities to learn and develop in ways that best suit them as individuals. ICT has the potential for being finely differentiated and providing individualised, sensitive feedback; therefore it can be particularly effective in helping to close the opportunity gap for children with additional support needs.

1. We will ensure that we meet the needs of SEN children through our SEN policy which aims to enable all children to access the curriculum through a positive approach.

   Specially designed equipment such as touch screens, switches and appropriate software enable such access.

We are also concerned that the ergonomics of computer access is appropriate to children with disabilities.

2. We will support and value cultural identities and diversity by using the internet appropriately.

3. The use of ICT applications to enable non-verbal children to access the whole of the curriculum will be achieved through visual aids created by staff, shared with parents and used at home and nursery.

4. We will take up opportunities ICT offers to become involved in partnership with parents and with local and wider communities.

5. Children with SEN will usually be given one to one teaching to enable them to access the curriculum through ICT.

6. Gifted and talented children will be identified as early as possible through our assessment procedures and encouraged to reach their potential through specially devised programmes of learning. ICT will be used for recording assessments, target setting and data analysis. These children's use of ICT will be especially encouraged so their capabilities and motivation are developed.

Liaison, transfer and transition between settings

1. Factual information about children and families transferring between settings will be recorded on the Phoenix data system used by Derbyshire LEA

2. Administrative DCC software will enable staff to record and make assessments for children with special educational needs according to the Code of Practice. It will be used for IEPs and statement applications and passed onto settings.

3. Target-setting data about individual children's assessments will be recorded on Microsoft Excel and shared with the advisory service, governors, all staff and primary schools.

4. The Social Services data base will be accessed from one specified computer in the centre and information concerning children in need will be provided through this system as a child is transferred from one setting to the next.

5. An ICT co-ordinator will work with the primary schools, specifically the reception teachers and teaching assistants, to ensure continuity of the children's progress.

6. The use of ICT to develop special equipment for non-verbal children will be shared with schools, to enable these children to continue using systems which are appropriate and familiar. Other ICT resources to enable children with a special need to access the curriculum will be purchased or made.

Staff development

All teachers have accessed the NOF staff development training programme and completed it successfully.

A programme of training will be undertaken by all staff to increase skills and knowledge so they can use ICT for planning, teaching, record keeping, communication and access to further knowledge.

All staff may access training provided by the LEA or other outside agencies.

Julie Meaton is the staff development co-ordinator.

Partnership with parents

We intend to use ICT applications in our communications with our parents whenever appropriate. As examples we will undertake the following:

- ■ use the interactive white board for messages, videos, still photos, web sites

- ■ use desk top publishing to make handbooks, newsletters, brochures etc attractive and interesting

- ■ share and make videos for parents

- ■ use digital photos for records, visits, cards, books etc to give to parents

- ■ to use ICT to make games for children to use at home

- ■ make singing CD's, talking books etc for children to take home

- ■ ask parents to trial software

- ■ create work shops for parents in ICT, videoing etc

Communication and Early Excellence programme of dissemination

The centre has a web site – www.gamesleyeec.org.uk. Updating the web site is the responsibility of Cathy Jones, the ICT co-ordinator.

The centre has the responsibility of disseminating good ICT practice in the Foundation stage to other practitioners and has been given DfES funding to achieve this.

A pack of training materials consisting of videos, powerpoint presentations, resources and handouts is available to be delivered to other early years establishments and schools.

Visitors are also encouraged to the centre to look at ICT practice.

Health and Safety

Health and safety procedures regarding computer use and use of electrical equipment will be adhered to as set out in the health and safety policy, e.g. timing of computer use incorporating a break, ergonomics, testing of electrical equipment.

Each member of staff accepts the responsibility for the health and safety of pupils in their care.

Appropriate legislation

1. All staff will be trained on the current legislation of the following:

    ■ use of the internet
    ■ data protection
    ■ health and Safety issues concerning ICT use
    ■ retrieval of information in the case of a disaster
    ■ access to information via ICT

Responsibilities

Carole Bennett is the ICT co-ordinator

Cathy Jones manages the web site, supports early years practitioners, and creates software

Joanne Lowe is the co-ordinator for Knowledge and Understanding of the World

Carolyn Revell Hughes is the information and training officer

7

Case Study 2
The Northamptonshire ICT Strategy

The Northamptonshire ICT Strategy (NICTS) was launched in 2003 with a budget commitment of £1.5 million to 2006. This initiative has been developed in collaboration with the Local Education Authority's nine nursery schools with the aim of ultimately providing for the full range of Northamptonshire foundation stage providers. The foundations for the strategy were developed in 2001/2 with major initiatives supporting ICT in the nursery schools and classes that led to teachers reporting positive learning impacts in all areas of the Early Learning Curriculum (Ager and Kendall, 2003). The Strategy provides an ICT entitlement for all Reception year pupils to be provided with 30 minutes a week of adult supported ICT activity, mostly delivered through small group activities, plus additional time for consolidation and practice. The entitlement specifies a recommended minimum of 10 per cent of all teaching and learning time involving ICT integrated across the curriculum. References are also made to entitlements related to diversity and equality of access, parental involvement, enhanced assessment and recording and the support of trained practitioners. All this is has been backed up by significant training and material resources to support the strategy. For 2003-6 a basic allocation of £1,600 has been provided for each Lead Reception Class with an additional £70.00 per pupil. Additional funding of up to £5000 per school has been made available, along with funding for 3-8 days of supply cover. In the past year, Lead Reception Teachers (LRTs) have been playing a key role in developing their own practice as well as a range of skills to be employed throughout the continued term of the strategy to support schools in their local clusters. Over the next two years it is intended that this process will continue and extend the support, sharing good practice with all the non-maintained foundation stage settings as well.

Our evaluation of this initiative has aimed to show the extent to which the Strategy:

- changed practices in the classroom

- has been perceived to have improved pupil learning and motivation

- has influenced change in teachers beliefs, attitudes and understanding of ICTs

- has enhanced the school climate to promote a positive ICT learning environment

- has changed parental interest and involvement in their child's education.

The evaluation also aimed to support the strategy by working with LRTs in designing their own self evaluation systems and the evaluation objectives were to:

1. provide a formative component in the evaluation which would include collection of data by teachers and dissemination of findings at regular intervals to influence practice development within and between schools

2. where appropriate, to use objective measures to demonstrate any success of the ICT Strategy

3. to evaluate whether the associated training had any impact and what could be learned from this

4. to understand and monitor the use of ICT in the Foundation Stage and the understandings of ICT amongst practitioners, children and parents

5. to work collaboratively with teachers and schools to monitor children's and practitioners' learning.

Methodology

Data were collected from the 18 LRTs through teacher questionnaires, and through the analysis of action plans, project diaries, case study reports and relevant school evaluations.

The LRTs were given training, methods and resources to collect appropriate and similar information for their own school and to support the cluster schools, e.g.

- The ICT Early Childhood Environmental Sub-scale (ECERS-ICT)
- Access and control of ICT tools
- Information and Communication Handling Skills
- Learning about the uses of ICT
- ICT Application Reviews
- Semi-structured practitioner and headteacher interview schedule
- Parent questionnaire

We also conducted ratings and independent observations and triangulated these with teachers' data.

In the process of this collaborative and formative evaluation we provided detailed information and training on recent research on effective pedagogy in the Foundation Stage, excellence in ICT's usage, and effective teaching and learning. The LRTs and nursery school representatives were introduced to the latest research findings on effective learning and quality ICT practice. These included references to the Effective Provision of Pre-school Education (EPPE) project, the Researching Effective Pedagogy in the Early Years (REPEY) project, the European Commission funded Developmentally Appropriate Technology in Early Childhood (DATEC) project, IBM's European KidSmart programme evaluation, as well as relevant findings from the Economic and Social Research Council (ESRC) Teaching and Learning Research Programme (TLRP).

Exemplars of good practice were also provided and these were drawn from case study material collected from the Gamesely Early Excellence Centre and from resource bases associated with our prior experience with DATEC, BECTA, and DfES research. The LRTs and nursery representatives were introduced to the ICT Early Childhood Environmental Rating (ICT-ECERS subscale) subscale and shown how this could be applied for the purposes of self-assessment and school improvement. The LRTs were also given support in conducting a parent survey and suggestions were made on how they might develop their work following any report back to parents.

The LRTs were then able to report upon and share their analysis of the parent questionnaires and their ICT application reviews. They were given support in compiling reflective diaries and producing case studies, many of which have been drawn upon throughout this text. It was agreed that the reflective diaries should, as far as possible, include:

- Day-to-day reflections
- ICT resources
- Staff development, parent involvement
- Displays, videos and digital photos
- Children's activities – evidence of learning
- School ICT development plans
- ICT policy, current and development
- Dissemination work within school and as LRTs to other schools.

The case studies might for instance report on work related to a single child's ICT learning, a particular interest group, SEN, gender, EAL or re-port on in-depth evaluation of a single ICT application.

The evaluators visited all the schools in June 2004 to observe current practice and to hold discussions with LRTs, headteachers and ICT co-ordinators. The baseline ICT ECERS subscale ratings were therefore supported by independent observations by the principal evaluators and also triangulated with teachers' data. These 1:1 sessions with the LRTs provided another opportunity to discuss their analysis of the parent survey data and how they planned to report back to parents, their reflec-tive diaries, portfolios of children's work, the case studies, application reviews and their planned work with cluster schools/nurseries.

Throughout the period a major programme of training sessions was provided by the LEA Advisory Team:

1. ICT – Putting the Principles of Early Years Education into practice

The aim of this session was to draft Early Years Principles for all the Lead Schools to work from. It was considered important that the schools worked together and with the advisory team to produce this. Seven prin-ciples were collaboratively agreed, covering: The learning environment; parental involvement; continuity and progression; role of the adult; planning; observation and assessment; and effective learning.

2. Appropriate use of interactive whiteboards

This session examined the appropriate use of interactive whiteboards. The session began with a discussion of the potential health and safety issues and how to decide where to site the board. The rest of the session was hands-on, exploring the use of software on an interactive white-board. Each of the activities was evaluated to decide if it offered the most appropriate way of achieving the declared learning intentions.

3. Developing an understanding of everyday technologies through role play and electronic toys

This session examined how children's understanding of everyday technology could be developed through socio-dramatic role play and how role play could be enhanced through the use of ICT.

4. Enhancing learning and teaching through the use of a computer and programmable toys

The group discussed the seven agreed principles and then engaged in a hands-on session to explore the software available. Different aspects and affordances of each of the educational tools and toys were demonstrated. Throughout, the participants considered whether the activities were the most appropriate way of achieving their learning intentions.

5. Appropriate use of digital photography and video to enhance learning and teaching

The session began with a brief discussion of the health and safety issues, followed by discussion on the power of using digital photography for learning and teaching. The rest of the session was hands on and explored how photographs and video can be used in their own right and when used within different applications in particular:

- Tizzy's First Tools
- Word
- PowerPoint
- Easiteach

6. Using ICTs as tools to enhance teaching and learning

Starting from a set of medium term plans the participants explored how ICT could be used to enhance learning and teaching. The session aimed to develop understanding that planning must start with the learning intention and then consider how ICT tools might be employed to achieve it. The session was intended to provide an antidote to the usual approach to purchasing a new ICT tool: 'Now that I've got this, what do I use it for?'

Members of the LEA Early Years Advisory Team also visited each school once, to provide any additional support required. Each Lead School was also funded to provide one open day per half-term at which up to a total of four Year 1 or 2 Cluster practitioners can attend in the morning and four in the afternoon. In addition, each pair of Lead Schools were jointly to plan and deliver an evening training session each half-term for practitioners from Year 1 Cluster Schools in the Spring term and Year 1 and 2 Cluster Schools in the Summer term.

The evaluation forms completed at the end of each of these sessions show that they were extremely well received. Ninety three per cent of participants reported that the course was either 'excellent' or 'good' in terms of meeting its objectives. Particular strengths noted included the opportunities offered to explore new equipment and applications, the opportunities for open discussion, the expertise and clear explanations from the advisory team, and the use of video clips and handouts. The opportunity to provide feedback directly to the NICTS team was also much appreciated. Many of the participants also reported on their intentions to follow up on these sessions in their classrooms. The themes which predominated were:

- developing more high quality socio-dramatic role play (that included and was supported by ICTs)

- planned application of a wide range of new ICTs hardware and software

Formative Feedback

The evaluators provided the first formative feedback to the LRTs in May 2004, reporting on both the ICT ECERS baseline scores and the initial survey findings from teachers, head teachers and parents. The school visits provided an opportunity to discuss their individual school ICT-ECERS subscale rating with each LRT. It was explained that although a number of items on the standardised scale might not fit into their immediate development plans for ICT, there might be others they would wish to prioritise. Nursery school scores were reported to individual nurseries by post.

Further feedback in December 2004 included a report based on our (Siraj-Blatchford J and I, 2004b) observations of the settings and on the policy analysis. Each LRT was provided with individual feedback on their reflective diaries and their progress as recorded by our ICT-ECERS observations. In May 2005 a final report recorded the progress made according to the end of evaluation ICT-ECERS subscale ratings, the end of year evaluation questionnaires completed by LRTs and head teachers, and upon the analysis of the first three months' work reported in the LRT project diaries. It was intended that this feedback would continue opportunities for the LRTs to learn from the evaluation findings and optimise their dissemination strategies accordingly. Special conditions for the use of images, including those featuring children, were agreed and the LRTs had gathered together significant training resources of their own.

Findings

From the start, the results of our observations and assessment of the quality of the ICT learning environment using the ICT subscale were encouraging. The level of support and the funding provided by Northamptonshire LEA has been exceptional and the results achieved were extraordinarily good. Figure 15 shows the baseline reception class scores for each of the three ICT ECERS subscale items related to; Learning about the uses of ICT; Information and Communication Handling Skills, and Access and control of ICT tools.

Figure 15

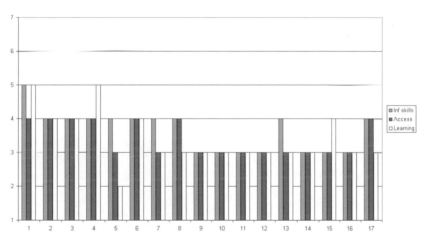

Figure 16

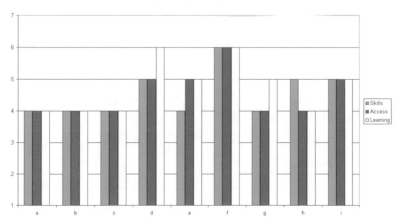

Average ECERS-ICT Subscale Scores Reception and Nurseries March 2004

Figure 17

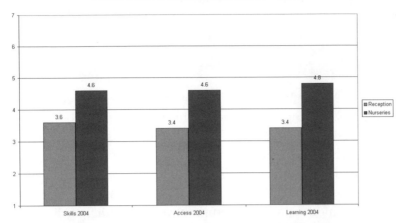

Figure 16 shows how these scores compare to the scores obtained from Nurseries who had already benefited from involvement in the Foundation stage ICT strategy:

Figure 17 shows a comparison between the average scores found in this baseline evaluation early in 2004:

The average baseline scores for all the Northamptonshire settings involved in the evaluation were:

Table 9

	Nursery School	Reception
Items from the ICT subscale		
Information handling and Communication Skills	4.5	3.6
Access and control of ICT tools	4.5	3.4
Learning about the uses of ICT	4.8	3.4

To put these scores into context we can compare them with the ratings achieved by a sample of UK pre-schools who received training and computer hardware and software resources through IBMs KidSmart programme in 2002/3:

Table 10

Items from the ICT subscale	Pre- intervention	final visit
Information handling and Communication Skills	2.7	4.9
Access and control of ICT tools	2.1	5.2
Learning about the uses of ICT	2.3	4.8

The Northamptonshire nurseries had higher average ICT-ECERS scores than those found in the reception classes and little of the practice observed in reception classes could match the high quality of the two best nurseries. The nurseries had already benefited from sustained support with resources and training and many have collaborated closely in the ongoing development of the NICT Foundation Stage strategy.

Figure 18 shows the ICT subscale scores achieved by the LRTs by the end of the evaluation period.

Throughout the year the Nursery classes were also developing their practice but as Figure 19 shows, the progress the Reception Classes made, as compared to the Nurseries, has been quite exceptional.

Figure 18

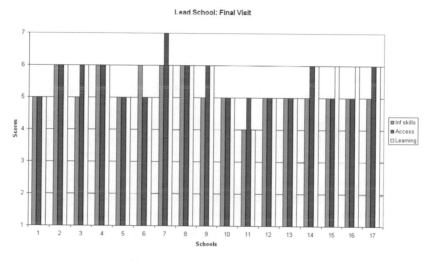

Figure 19

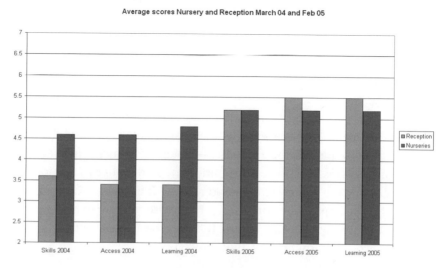

The ICT Curriculum

The baseline LRT responses to the question; 'How do you understand the term Information and Communications Technology?' were revealing (see Figure 20). They compare well with responses found in other Early Years surveys, which have often suggested an overemphasis on desktop computers. The responses suggest some fluency with the commonly applied LEA definitions of the term.

Figure 20

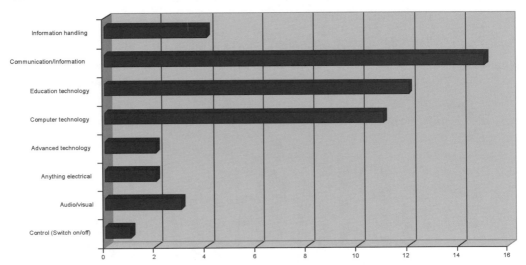

At the end of the year all but one of the LRTs reported that their understanding of ICT had changed significantly. In nearly every case they noted that their perceptions had become broader and how important they now believed the subject to be. The following response was typical:

> I am considerably more aware of constantly bringing ICT to the attention of the children and showing them what a huge impact it has on everyday life. We look far beyond Computers, cameras and telephones now to encompass ICT everywhere! (LRT 12).

In the baseline survey, the teachers were also asked what, if anything, they thought children learned from using the computer. Here again the responses were encouraging from the start. While most early years practitioners tended to emphasise the technical skills involved for children in learning how to operate the computer – using the mouse, hand-eye co-ordination etc – many of the LRTs mentioned a wide range of curriculum areas including the 'nature of technology itself' (Figure 21). At the end of the year this had broadened out even further with references being made in nearly every case to the use of ICTs across the curriculum. LRTs referred to socio-dramatic play. Typically:

114

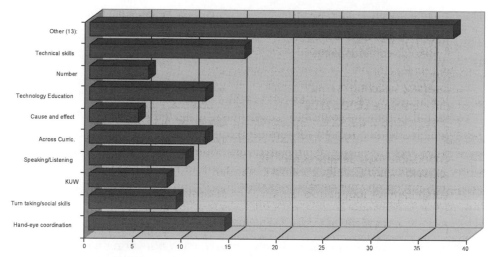

Figure 21

My understanding has changed, as I now see the communication part of the subject much more important. It has also widened my knowledge of the subject and I have used much more ICT in imaginative play where before the project, the ICT tended to be just using the computer. (LRT 6)

I now use a much wider range of ICTs (interactive whiteboard, programmable toys, digital cameras, tape recorders, musical keyboards, remote control cars) and integrate them into the children's play. This has partly been due to the availability of resources, the training I have received and a greater understanding of how children learn through ICTs by working more closely with them – some 'sustained shared thinking' I hope. (LRT 4)

Previous studies often show that teachers answer the question 'How is the computer used to assist in the teaching of Early Learning Goals?' quite differently – and this was borne out in the teachers' baseline responses (Figure 22).

Figure 21

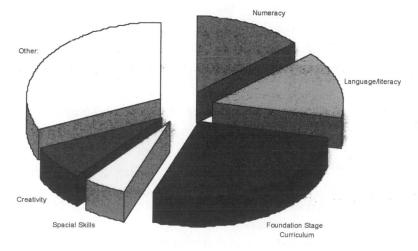

How is the computer used to assist in teaching Early Learning Goals?

The difference in responses to these two questions is probably due partly to the teachers' assumptions about the importance of basic and foundation skills, and the overall educational purpose/justification of the computer. But it is clear that the answer to the first question is based on observations rather than intentions and that this difference is problematic. We needed to move towards a situation where the responses match up. Teachers need to observe the children's learning at the computer more closely related to different areas of the CGFS. Only when they become more aware of this learning (or its absence) will they be able to engage in the process of supporting and scaffolding it. The end of year responses show progress along these lines with 10 (59 per cent) of the 17 LRTs providing essentially the same response to each question.

Adult support at the computer

The *Effective Provision of Pre-school Education* (EPPE) (Sylva *et al*, 2004), and *Researching Effective Pedagogy in Early Childhood* (REPEY) (Siraj-Blatchford *et al*, 2002) studies found that the most effective foundation stage settings combined the provision of free play opportunities with more focused group work involving adult instruction. The EPPE/REPEY research also suggested that adult-child interactions involving some element of sustained shared thinking were especially valuable in terms of children's early learning.

But a number of studies have found that pre-school educators are rarely present when children are computing. Even when qualified teachers are present, adult support is rarely longer than two or three minutes. In the majority of cases, adult support is limited to intervention when the children experience problems or require supervision. It seems that most children are left to develop their computing skills independently, with pre-school educators questioning, instructing and managing only when necessary.

The amount of time that teachers or other adults sit with children at the computer was found to be very low in the baseline survey, although not as low as has been found in other studies, even where the adult:child ratios were somewhat better. Table 11 shows a comparison of the baseline findings with those found in an evaluation of the IBM KidSmart programme in the UK (Siraj-Blatchford, J and I, 2004a). The table also shows that the situation in the reception classes is improving as practitioners make less use of computer suites and more of their new Interactive whiteboards.

Table 11

per cent of time	0-20%	21-40%	41-60%	61-80%	81-100%
NICTS Baseline	68	24	6	0	2
NICTS End of year	35	35	25	13	0
IBM(UK)	75	19	0	0	6

In fact the interactive whiteboards are valued extremely highly. As LRT 4 and LRT 5 have reported:

> 30.6.04: Felt brave enough to use the data projector today – the children were absolutely thrilled, comments along the lines of 'wow', 'wicked' and 'its really big'. I used Izzy's Island and immediately discovered the value of the whiteboard. Sitting at the computer I was able to seat the whole class, all 27, where they could see clearly, I could face them and have a dialogue about choices and decisions in using the programme. I love the interactive whiteboard! (LRT 4, Reflective Diary)

> ...Used the whiteboard to share ORT talking stories with the children. It went well. I have some children on the autistic spectrum in my class and I was finding it difficult to get them to settle during story time. They managed to focus much more on the whiteboard than on me! So I will try to use it for a talking story once a week until they are more able to sit quietly and attentively. They also respond with very obvious enjoyment to music, so will also use the CD player at group time regularly. On the down side, I am having to turn the computers and whiteboard off before they come back to our base because they find it impossible to walk past them to get to carpet time. (LRT 5, Reflective Diary)

Feeling comfortable with the computer

Many of the teachers who responded to the baseline survey felt less comfortable with the computer in their classroom than colleagues in some other LEA foundation stage settings. Seventy percent of the teachers in Northampton reported being 'comfortable' with the computer and 15 per cent 'very comfortable', compared to 40 per cent found to be comfortable and 62 per cent very comfortable (following training) in the UK IBM sample. This situation has now improved with 50 per cent of the LRTs saying they are 'comfortable' and 50 per cent 'very comfortable'. There are still, however, some major frustrations and many of the teachers reported on the technical problems they have experienced and the disruption caused through delays in dealing with them.

Have a lot of trouble with the (LEA website) this week. Have managed to ask (Adviser) for access to the folder for lead teachers but can't get back in to get reply. It is so frustrating and such a waste of time when things do not work properly!! Hope that the e-mail will be back on-line next week. (LRS 5, Reflective Diary)

A great deal of frustration was expressed in the early stages when equipment was first delivered and installed and it was felt that much of this could have been avoided through more careful planning and greater communication.

23.9. 04: Frustration, the training we had with Tizzy's Toolbox is virtually useless as the programme that has been installed on both my computers does not work. Rang (hardware supplier) about this who said it's a problem with the Sherston software not compatible with the new machines! ...No one seems to take responsibility for it and everyone seems to pass the buck! (LRT 9, Reflective Journal)

24.5.04-28.5.04: My topic this term has been mini-beasts. This week I made a garden outside with plants, paths, a bucket of water for the pond etc. Pixie was dressed as a ladybird and was to be moved around the garden by the children. On Monday morning Pixie refused to work and despite attempts by several members of staff it was out of action all week. This meant that a large part of my planned lessons did not take place. The children were disappointed and I was more so because I have not carried out such an activity before and was looking forward to seeing the children's reactions. (LRT 16, Reflections)

Week 6: Very poor installation service – engineers only able to mount onto the wall – not fully trained to connect up or install software. Luckily Barbara managed to come to the rescue so I pity the schools that do not have an ICT specialist on the staff. Some doubt now whether stage needed – spoke to (Adviser) today who said hang fire as she is deter- Image 34

mined that supplier will come back to re-mount projectors and whiteboard at child friendly heights – contractors say not possible because of height of projector – adviser says it can be done with correct mounting. (LRT 11b, Weekly Diary)

5.10.04: What a nightmare! Can things get any worse? Was acting head today and had *all* 31 of my reception in this morning but spent most of the morning on the phone to supplier and adviser, arguing the height of the board. What is the point of having a whiteboard if the children can't reach it? Finally after 3 hours I spoke to supplier who agreed to lower the board to 40cms from the floor as long as I put it in writing that I am not happy with the height of the board, the school will pay for a call out and technician. I agreed as I had had enough!!! Then to top it all, all afternoon I couldn't get it working to my computer... (LRT 9, Reflective Journal)

This practitioner later reported gaining greater confidence and experiencing significant success with the whiteboard despite these initial teething problems. Though feeling out of her depth with the technology at times, she thought that when all was working properly the benefits outweighed the problems:

All children have a sense of achievement and I have seen a lot of children doing what I call 'the victory dance', when they are so thrilled with themselves they dance and show off to the other children! It is wonderful to see... (LRT 9, Reflections, 12.04).

Policy developments

All the schools had an ICT policy but the baseline headteacher survey showed that only half of the schools currently differentiate in their policy between the needs of children over and under 5.

Where they differentiated:

3 schools referred to Foundation Stage/ELGs
2 schools referred to the use of different software applications
1 schools referred to the curriculum being more exploratory
1 school referred to the curriculum being more play based

In seven of the seventeen Lead schools, ICT policies were revised as a result of the NICTS initiative, each referring to specific references to indicate the different approach being taken in the foundation stage. The following approach is typical:

Distinct section on the Foundation Stage provision – highlighting approach to ICTs in reception – acknowledging its exploratory basis in play to support learning. The policy also now recognises the wide variety of ICT resources (real and pretend). (LRT 15)

In all but two of the cases where the policies have not been revised, the LRTs reported that their policy would soon be revised.

Provision for play

A good range of software was available in many reception classrooms but little was integrated in quality play provision/contexts. A good deal of literacy/numeracy drill and practice was observed early in 2004 and play in general was very varied in the reception classes. But there was a dearth of either pretend or real ICT for this and imagination was lacking – little pretend ICT was created in the setting. Staff were convinced about the value of ICT in play but little was seen that was in any way sustained. As the ICT-ECERS subscale results show, this situation has changed markedly. For many of the LRTs the development of socio-dramatic play has been challenging. But the creativity of many of the applications they developed was impressive (see Chapter 1), as was the quality of the critical reflections that came with them:

> ...From a professional development point of view this case study has made me much more aware of how I can use ICT in a more 'integrated' manner within the classroom and has highlighted the value of role-play in providing such opportunities. It has also given me greater confidence in using a range of ICT resources, such as the PC Tablet which is relatively new to the school. (LRT 15b, Case Study)

> I was particularly satisfied with the success of the video and the internet stimulus, not just on their language, but also in modeling the real uses of the ICTs. This immediately gave the resources value and meaning in the play setting, which remained over time. (LRT 15a, Case Study)

Ergonomics

When we first visited the schools, most computer screens – in the reception classes particularly – were too high for children to view comfortably. Some settings had addressed this by putting the monitor alongside or under the base unit and on tables of the correct height. There was still widespread use of a full size mouse. No expert advice appears to be currently available regarding the safety of using interactive whiteboards with children under 5. BECTA provides advice which includes warnings of a potential though limited risk to eyesight but it is not clear whether this applies to the latest projectors, nor whether the risks are the same for young as for older children. Though these concerns about the possible effects of interactive whiteboards thus remained unresolved, there was significant improvement in other respects. Schools have given particular attention to the height of tables and the size of the mouse being used by children. Some schools had tables custom-made locally. One or two whiteboards remained too high for the children to access easily although this has now been resolved.

Resources

Resource provision in terms of computers and related hardware were generally good (significantly better than found in other foundation stage settings) and every setting had at least one working modern computer, most had more, and some had access to several. Some reception classes had timetabled access to a computer suite. Some settings had already been equipped with interactive whiteboards, although a few were either not working or still awaiting installation. Access to programmable toys was more varied, although most had one or two 'in the cupboard'. All this has been greatly improved, although frustrations with regard to delays in computer servicing persist and there are also problems about the repair of non-computer ICT equipment.

The opportunity to make their own choice of resources was much appreciated by many of the LRTs and it was clear from a number of comments that this was taken very seriously:

> ...this is a huge responsibility and I want to have time to research products and audit thoroughly what we need. (LRT 1, Reflections)

Many found the time spent researching into resources and finding the best price time consuming. Some felt it would have been useful to have had the opportunity for hands-on experience with the resources before purchase. Some teachers reported that the impact of the initiative was being felt throughout their school:

> The training and resources have made a big difference. It will have a knock-on effect up the school. Colleagues have questioned their provision and asked 'If they are doing that in Reception, what will they be able to do when they come to me?' (LRT 7, Final Report)

> Due to the increase in skills at the foundation stage the objectives for year 1 to 6 have had to be adjusted to accommodate the improved skills of the younger children. (LRT 16)

Formative assessment and reflective diaries

Many of the entries found in the reflective diaries demonstrate sustained focus on individual children and/or particular ICT applications. Many of these observations were formative.

Both the case studies and the notes in LRT reflective diaries show that lead teachers are closely monitoring the development of the children's ICT skills and understandings. References to the practical responses to these formative assessments are frequent:

> ...it has been wonderful to witness a child's natural curiosity into how things work grow and develop and having the resources to give him that experience is wonderful! The use of pretend ICTs however has given me a greater understanding of his knowledge about how things work and to plan for his future learning. (LRT 9, Case Study Child 3)

> ...X had been having problems with his turn on the computer. He always wanted to be in control using the mouse and selecting the programme. He wanted to work with his friends but did not have the skills and often became frustrated. Through adult interaction and support, praise and positive reminders, he is now becoming more adept at sharing and taking turns. He now realises he will have plenty of goes on the computer and that sharing makes using the computer more enjoyable. As a result he is now better at sharing with his peers during other activities. (LRT 3, Case Study)

The following were typical of the quality of observations recorded in the reflective diaries. They also show how many featured focused observations of individual children:

> 30.09.04: Many of the ICT resources have helped to capture, and hold, X's attention for increasing periods of time. He is not interacting very well with others in the class and is not keen to wait for his turn, which makes some of the other children less keen to include him in their play, particularly in the role play area (home corner, at present).

> 03.11.04: X is now constantly pointing out 'technology'.

> 16.11.04: The recent setting up of the interactive whiteboard [IWB] has helped X to develop some degree of patience, as he is now able to wait his turn to use it, when working in a group. This has been invaluable in boosting him with his peers. X is very good at recognising and adding numbers. When working with the whiteboard with number, for example, the size makes it possible for others to see how clever he is, which I am sure is helping with both his self-esteem and his standing, amongst his peers. It has also given him another avenue down which to devote his seemingly endless energy. Looking back over my notes, it is also possible to see that X is collaborating more with his peers and is less demanding of my attention. (LRT 14)

> 27.9.04: Y enjoyed using Izzy's Island today on the computer. IWB worked morning only then we had to use the mouse. Y likes the music and the characters. Tried each activity and stayed at computer, really absorbed, for some time (1/2 hour).
>
> 4.10.04: Really enjoyed using Tizzy's First Numbers today. New pen for IWB not solved the problem but he is happy to use the mouse and head-phones. Tends to get obsessed with one thing (security) so we have to try to make sure he is not in front of the computer too long. Went through every activity. Enjoys using Colour Magic and printing his work. Also likes Teddy Bears' Picnic. Again has gone through each activity – very absorbed and seems to know exactly what he is doing. (LRT 1, Reflections)

These formative assessment practices should be strongly supported. In the best practice practitioners kept portfolios of achievement (see Appendix A).

Home learning, parent partnership and the role of ICT

The findings of our study of home learning and ICT in Northamptonshire are reported in Chapter 4. Although any detailed analysis of the effects of home ICT use lay beyond the scope of the evaluation there were good reasons to suggest that when parents actively supported their children at the computer and in other ICT contexts we might expect similar benefits to those identified in the EPPE research. The LRTs were therefore asked to survey their parents to find out about their home learning environments and particularly about the children's access and use of ICTs.

Conclusions

The progress made by the LRTs has been excellent, and one school has been exceptional. Their policy developments are also particularly sophisticated – they have adopted a distinct play-based and 'emergent' approach to ICTs in the foundation stage:

> The strategy has changed my practice in the classroom, improved pupil learning and motivation, influenced change in my beliefs, attitudes and understandings of ICTs. It has given me the freedom to focus on the teaching pedagogy and not the resources I need to teach for some lessons... I feel empowered by the knowledge I have gained and in the new year, I will be organising workshops for parents, to highlight that ICT is not solely desktop computers and peripherals, and to encourage them to use the computer at home. (LRT 7, Case study)

Across all the schools, it seems that the quality of play experiences generally, not just those with a central focus on ICTs, have been improved by the initiative. Teachers have been re-energised by the project's focus on play and in several cases they have radically re-assessed what they provide.

In many ways and at every level the NICT strategy has encouraged greater awareness of the educational potential of ICT:

> I am particularly impressed with the self-correcting evaluation and change aspect of ICTs. Some of the programmes not only work at the children's level and move them forward but can alter the pace to fit in with their individual speed of learning, something even the best of teachers couldn't do continuously. (headteacher, LS 16)

> I felt that children have become much more confident in themselves. They have begun to take risks, explore and find out for themselves. They question more and take control of their own learning'. (LRT 9, Final Report)

Using the ICT-ECERS as a curriculum development tool has been particularly successful. From an early stage the LRTs were encouraged to make an objective assessment of their practice and to identify clear targets for development:

> 22.6.04: Visit from Iram to view setting, meet my maternity cover and feedback scores. Iram boosted my confidence no end with her enthusiasm, praise and positive comments. She was very helpful and gave clear sound advice. Our ECERS scores were good and we know where we're going to improve our practice. (LS 1, Reflections)

Some of the LRTs expressed dismay at the low scores awarded on the initial assessment, though nobody disputed them. They were determined to do better and show what they could do, particularly in the area of lCTs and play provision, which had been identified as a weakness in most classes.

The LRTs' emphasis on ICT Skills has improved but developments do lag a little behind access and learning. This is to be expected and they will catch up now that access is so good, and the learning is in the process of being internalised and consolidated. We have seen substantial increases in ICT-ECERS subscale scores across the board for nearly all the primaries. After just one year the scores for nursery and reception are now broadly comparable, with a slightly greater average for reception. There are two main reasons for this success. Firstly there has been a pro-

Image 35

gramme of training which has been valued by nearly all staff we spoke to and which has, in their judgement and in ours, contributed directly to the development of good practice. In addition to the actual content of this training, the opportunities to share and discuss with other participants was clearly of great benefit.

Secondly, there has been a dramatic improvement in resource levels, with all participants receiving much in the way of high quality ICT resources. This has transformed the ICT environment in the reception classes, giving many children access to interactive whiteboards, digital cameras and videos, laptops, powerful computers, microscopes, webcams etc for the first time. The range and quality of play ICT equipment has increased markedly. It is also good to see that often these are made in class in collaboration with the children.

The provision of new resources has acted as a catalyst for the development of the curriculum more generally. Both the training and the additional resources have been central to the improvements. Training on its own would have led to frustration and an inability to put the greater staff knowledge into practice. The resources without the training would have been used far less effectively. Teachers told us that they greatly valued the initial guidance they received in developing appropriate learning contexts, grounded firmly in good Early Years practice.

The developing awareness of ICTs being much wider than computers, and the concept of an ICT 'application' including both a 'tool' and a 'purpose' remain crucial to current and further development

We saw a few examples of children using the internet but there is still some fear among staff of what is 'out there'. In one school the teacher's parents went on a cruise. The children followed the ship's progress through the P&O website, had email updates from their teacher's parents and had a ship's bridge as their play theme. It was hoped a live webcam communication with the ship might be possible. Such experiences have substantial potential for enriching the educational experience of children. A number of schools have worked with parents and governors to develop their own Internet Access Policies.

There is an issue about what happens when the children go into Year I, and whether their reception experiences will be built on. Schools are aware that this is partly a management matter to do with continuity and progression but it also necessitates further training and resources in Y1.

In their final reports, each LRT identified the major areas of personal development and their future development plans. LRT 16, for example, referred to her increased awareness of the full range of ICTs and their use in role play. She clearly intends to provide for more of these experiences and to continue to update her knowledge of ICT. Frequent references were made to greater awareness of ICT and the impact of the NICTS initiative on developing the confidence, skills and understandings of teachers throughout the Lead schools. Many LRTs have plans for further specific purchases and for extending use of digital cameras. They wrote of encouraging the children to develop greater independence in their use of ICTs, of intentions to continue to seek out more information and training, and to tighten up ICT curriculum planning.

Only one LRT referred in her development planning to cluster group training, and only two specifically to working more closely with parents. These will need to be the primary focus of LEA support in the next phase of the strategy. Many of the LRTs do now see the potential of working with parents to improve home learning environments:

> Sometimes home environment is rich in technology and this is not followed up in school. Usually in poor socio-economic areas like ours computer software is no more than poor arcade type games. Powerful reason to demonstrate quality – need to plan for open evening in November. (LRT 7, Sept, 2004 Reflections)

In this, and in other areas, it will be important to monitor developments as the LRTs continue to develop and disseminate their good practice.

8
Case Study 3
IBM KidSmart Programme

The IBM KidSmart Initiative

The IBM KidSmart *Early Learning Programme* is a major example of corporate philanthropy which aims to help 'bridge the digital divide' by donating *Young Explorer*™ (*Little Tykes*) Computer Centres and Riverdeep software in non-profit pre-school settings serving disadvantaged communities around the world. Globally, IBM invested $7.5 million in the KidSmart Early Learning Programme, with 1,800 KidSmart Early Learning Centres donated in Europe across 19 countries over the three years to the end of 2002. Current plans are to donate another 15,000 units worldwide by the end of 2005, bringing the total units donated in the UK to 780. By then the programme will have expanded to more than 50 countries in Europe, Asia, Latin America and Africa.

As the first phase of their KidSmart programme in the UK, IBM donated 27 of their Early Learning Centres, complete with their educational software, to fourteen nurseries in 1999. As in other countries, IBM worked in partnership with a local organisation whose role was to identify appropriate recipient settings and to provide training and support. IBM chose Early Education (the British Association for Early Childhood Education) as its UK partner. They commissioned us to provide training, and to act as a point of contact for information, advice and support for the recipient centres. As the initiative rolled out further over the next two years and Local Education Authorities (LEAs) became involved, we provided LEA project liaison and maintained the project databases. These functions are now served by Early Education directly from its offices in Whitechapel, East London (see http://www.early-education.org.uk/). Early Education also commissioned us to provide an evaluation of the first phase of the UK programme in 2000-01 and we were subsequently commissioned by IBM to evaluate the programme in England, France, Germany, Spain and Italy over 2001-2003. The programme in the UK has now expanded to include 69 LEAs for whom we continue to provide training for trainers.

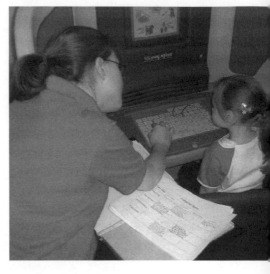

The UK KidSmart Evaluation

The Phase One study was conducted in the fourteen pre-school settings (four in Scotland and ten in England) that were initially identify as appropriate KidSmart recipients in the UK. Each offered a diversity of early childhood services in mainly disadvantaged areas. The settings included playgroups, nurseries, early excellence centres, family centres, and nursery classrooms.

Image 36

The study sought to investigate whether the IBM initiative had improved the information and communications technology (ICT) provision offered to the 3 and 4 year old children in the centres, and how the provision might be improved in the next phase of the project. The approach adopted in the study was informed strongly by the *Developmentally Appropriate Technology in Early Childhood* (DATEC) project, and by the position statement provided by NAEYC (the USA National Association for the Education of Young Children) for developmentally appropriate practices for children from birth through age 8. Both initiatives accept as a basic principle that all high quality early childhood programmes should 'provide a safe and nurturing environment that promotes the physical, social, emotional and cognitive development of young children while responding to the needs of families' (Bredekamp and Copple (1997). The design of the study was also informed by previous evaluations of

Image 37

the KidSmart programme that were carried out in the USA by Nancy Nager (1999 and 2000).

Nancy Nager's evaluations of the US KidSmart programme suggested that the following features of the US initiative had demonstrated strong evidence of programme improvement:

- the presence of adults working along-side the children at the computer

- the degree of 'comfort' reported by practitioners in having the Young Explorers in their classrooms

- the extent to which the computers are utilised.

- the extent to which the use of the computer is instructive, as demonstrated by the reduction of children's random clicking

- the extent to which children support each other at the computer

- the extent to which boys and girls are equally involved

- the extension of learning through e.g. adult questioning

- the level of knowledge practitioners demonstrate regarding the learning opportunities offered in the Edmark/Riverdeep software

- the level of satisfaction expressed by practitioners in the KidSmart training.

In addition to the above, our study addresses these general questions:

How effective has the KidSmart initiative been in developing Information and Communications Technology Education in the UK pre-school settings over the first year?

How 'developmentally appropriate' are the furniture, computer hardware and software for use by children in UK pre-schools?

How effective has the UK KidSmart training been, and what can be done to improve upon it in Phase 2?

Methodology

Non-equivalent but comparable control groups were studied alongside those selected for intervention. A pre-test provided the means by which the settings could be matched with a control setting comparable in terms of ICT provision. Two instruments initially developed for use in the DATEC project were used to collect data for the evaluation. The most elaborate of these is an Early Childhood Environment Rating Sub-Scale (ECERS) for ICT (see Chapter 6).

The other DATEC instrument was developed to review ICT applications (Appendix B), and another three instruments (Appendix C-E) have been developed to provide the remainder of the evaluation data identified above:

■ Semi-structured centre manager interview schedule: Each manager was interviewed at the start and end of this phase of the programme.

■ Practitioner Questionnaire: a total of 42 practitioner questionnaires were returned for analysis at the end of this phase.

■ Parent Questionnaire: questionnaires about the ICT home environment were returned and analysed (Reported in Chapter 4).

Pre-intervention site-visits were conducted in Autumn 2000 and the post-intervention visits in the summer of 2001. Initial DATEC training for the ICT co-ordinators in each setting was provided in December 2000. In addition a training visit was made to each of the settings approximately half way through the project to provide staff with an opportunity to critically review their practice, re-think assumptions and plan new activities. Exemplary work was identified and recorded for wider dissemination.

UK evaluation findings

Our most significant finding across all of the settings was that the children had clearly enjoyed, and the parents and practitioners had greatly appreciated, the improved access to ICT afforded by the KidSmart units. Our findings also showed that there significant improvements in every area of the ICT curriculum. When compared with our control group of settings, the findings suggest that the ICT provisions made in the KidSmart settings were initially broadly in line with other providers, and that after just one year 69 per cent of the KidSmart settings had achieved a rating of 'good' or better in at least one of the sub-scales. An improvement of two or more points was achieved in each area.

Table 12

ECERS Sub-scale, 3 items	'Control' (average)	Pre-intervention (average)	Post-intervention (average)
Learning about the Uses of ICT	2.2	2.6	4.6
Access and Control of ICT tools	1.5	1.7	4.1
Information Handling and Communication	2.5	1.9	4.3

We also asked the practitioners how 'comfortable' they felt about having the Young Explorers in their classrooms. Nager (1999) reported that after the first year approximately 25 per cent of the US practitioners were 'not too – but getting more comfortable' with the computers. At the end of the second year 51 per cent of these teachers reported that they were 'very comfortable' and 43 per cent that they were 'comfortable'. The situation seemed similar in the UK, many practitioners feeling some initial discomfort with the new technology but gaining in confidence as they built up experience.

At the start of the project none of the settings had an ICT curriculum development plan or a written policy. Half the settings developed ICT plans during the year and four of them developed ICT policies.

The practitioners reported on the equipment being used for between 50-90 per cent of the time and 50-100 per cent of this time was considered to be 'productive'. These figures appeared to be broadly in line with the US experience (Nager, 2000). But the variation we found in responses even from the same setting suggested that there was still a wide variation in understanding what might constitute a 'productive' use of the computer. As one practitioner put it:

> The children are always enthusiastic and keen to use computers. Even if programmes are not being used as intended the children are still commenting on pictures, colour etc.

In this first investigation we found that attitudes varied greatly towards the quality and quantity of supervision required. All but four of the practitioners and managers reported that 40 to 75 per cent of the children's time on the computer was closely supervised. One manager said that in her setting only 25 per cent of the time was supervised, and another practitioner claimed that 100 per cent was supervised.

Our initial interviews with setting managers showed that many took the term '*ICT education*' purely to mean computer education. Our interviews at the end of the year showed far more recognition of ICT as a broad term denoting all the technologies providing access to information and communication. Many of the settings evidenced substantial progress in using the ICT provision in socio-dramatic play and in involving the children more in operating the technology around them. In one setting, for example, children were involved for the first time in the design of new socio-dramatic play areas such as shops and offices, using pretend and real technology. And practitioners in one setting had taken children with them to discuss the programming of the washing machine used to launder the nursery aprons. Children from another setting observed checkout operators in a supermarket working with bar code scanners. On their return to the setting they identified the bar codes on a range of products and a pretend scanner was constructed for the children to play with (see Chapter 6).

Only through involvement in the KidSmart initiative did many of the settings learn how ICT might be integrated across the pre-school curriculum. In our initial interviews respondents referred exclusively to the integration of computers with a limited range of curriculum subjects.

When we asked them what they thought children learned from their use of the computer, their responses concentrated on the learning most directly associated with fine motor (mouse) skills and social interaction with and around the equipment. The study showed that most children worked together in pairs at the computer, although larger groups were also common. The data also suggested that the children took turns and collaborated when they were together at the computer although many of the practitioners' comments indicated some variation in understanding of the term 'collaboration' and there appeared to be a good deal of potential for further development in this area. As one setting manger reported:

> They cluster around it. I would say that it is not programmed in well to fit within the curriculum. It is generally overseen by members of staff but it is not to my mind as an integral part of the curriculum and I would like to develop that. The children are enthusiastic and they want to play with the computer. Those that have experience from home help others and what I would really like to see is children working together around the computer, the screen and the keyboard rather than isolating themselves.

Seventy per cent of our respondents suggested that boys and girls were gaining equal access to the computers. But in 30 per cent of cases, the boys were felt to be gaining more access and most practitioners were anxious to address this. The manager of one setting argued that it was a good thing that the boys dominated the computer because the nursery had little else to offer them. He argued that the nursery philosophy and environment was influenced strongly by women and that most activities such as dressing up were much more motivating for the girls. This manager was concerned about the educational underachievement of boys and saw the computer as offering real potential in terms of compensation.

We also asked managers and practitioners about their favourite software at the start and end of this phase of the programme. Where computers were already in use in the settings, a broad range of software was used. At the end of the year the KidSmart Riverdeep software emerged as by far the most commonly used, with *Millie's Math House* (especially *Build a Bug*), *Baileys Book House, Sammie's Science House* and *Trudy's Time and Place House* (especially the *Jelly Bean Hunt*) all specifically referred to. The other clear favourites were *Leaps and Bounds* (Brilliant Computing), *My World*, and *Switch on Travel* (Granada), and *Tizzy's Toybox* (Sherston). When we asked them about the criteria they applied in selecting software, most mentioned suitability for children's particular age/stage/ability; the quality of graphics; children's preferences, and the degree to which the activities provided were open ended.

Most of the practitioners believed children achieved much more in the setting if they had a computer at home, and only two practitioners said that although it gave them an 'initial' advantage, the others picked things up quickly. One practitioner wasn't sure. When we asked them in what way the children benefited from their experience at home, 43 per cent referred to 'mouse skills', 30 per cent to their skill and independence in accessing programmes, and 18 per cent to increased confidence.

We also asked the managers and practitioners how they thought the computer might contribute to achieving the Early Learning Goals (or the Scottish learning targets). Interestingly, these responses were quite different from their comments about the most likely learning outcomes, emphasising literacy, numeracy, colours and shapes this time.

The equipment proved itself both durable and effective. While a few of the settings had already obtained computer equipment before their involvement with KidSmart, this was mostly obtained second hand and offered little appropriate software. In one setting we were informed that they had a computer but that the speakers were not working and 'the children were better at using it than the staff'. In another we were told:

> Well we have within the family centre a development plan that includes ICT for the office-based staff but we haven't got a development plan on ICT for the nursery. We have had computers down in the nursery that were donated three years ago but they didn't last too long. They were used by children of different ages but I suppose they didn't have the appropriate training to use them properly.

These settings were especially impressed by the way the children have recognised and accepted the *Young Explorer* furniture as an appropriate part of their pre-school play environment.

Image 38 shows children being supported by an adult in one of the UK settings. The Young Explorer bench was designed to provide seating for two children and, according to the (US) documentation, 'scaled to place the monitor right at the child's eye level while the mouse and keyboard is within easy reach of little arms.'

Image 38

Unfortunately for the vast majority of the 3 and 4 year-old children attending the UK settings, the bench was found to be too low. The height of children in the 3 to 6 age group vary widely – charts produced by the US National Centre for Health Statistics (2000) suggest that this may be by as much as eleven inches. The ergonomics of sitting at a computer is therefore always a problem and, whatever the equipment provided, young children are often seen straining their necks looking upwards towards a screen. We have argued that this problem is best addressed by:

■ encouraging greater integration of the computer into activities demanding time away from it, and

■ talking to the children about healthy posture, so educating them from an early age about computer ergonomics, and encouraging them to use cushions when appropriate.

The mouse supplied with the KidSmart units was too big for little hands so a mini-mouse replacement was requested. IBM responded promptly with appropriate replacements. Image 39 shows a child in a German pre-

Image 39

school using an adult size mouse. The size is widely acknowledged as an ergonomic problem for young children. The Young explorer was fitted with a flat membrane keyboard developed for easy cleaning but some of the settings found this too sensitive. A significant number of practitioners also felt strongly that the children should be using a lower case keyboard. Again IBM responded promptly, providing lower case keyboards.

Most of the settings had not yet gained access to the internet so could not access support information or other early childhood sites. Reasons for this delay varied but in some cases the problem was clearly the cost of extending and/or providing additional telephone lines. There were also managers who had yet to realise the value or potential of obtaining access.

Nager's (2000) evaluation reported upon the level of satisfaction expressed by practitioners in the KidSmart training. Thirty two per cent of the US teachers found the training they received 'very helpful' and 19 per cent 'somewhat helpful'; only 2 per cent found them 'a little helpful'. In the UK, the KidSmart training was the only training many of the practitioners received. Most found it 'somewhat helpful' but some of the practitioners felt strongly that the kind of training they really needed at this stage was about developing basic computer skills rather than addressing either the potential of the Riverdeep software or the development of an effective early years ICT curriculum:

> I enjoyed being part of the IBM training even though I haven't learned anything. I prefer someone to come in the school and show us the capabilities of the computer.

Four of the settings came into the project late and although the centre managers or ICT co-ordinators attended some of the IBM sessions, they had joined the project too late to receive the DATEC on-site training at the time. This gave us an opportunity to evaluate the effectiveness of the centre based training. We found that the setting managers who received no on-site training did not show equivalent gains in their ECERS ICT sub-scale scores.

While most practitioners expressed an appreciation of the ICT curriculum training overall, there was clearly a need to provide more basic computer skills training at an early stage. This finding was acted upon in the second phase of the UK KidSmart donations by entering into partnership with local authorities who agreed to provide the basic training. LEAs also agreed to identify a member of their staff to attend a KidSmart national 'training the trainers' session and to feed back the ICT curriculum development training to their local settings. These developments constituted the first response of many LEAs to the ICT needs of the pre-school sector.

The European evaluation

The extension study was commissioned and funded by IBM, and initially provided an evaluation of the KidSmart programme in five European countries: France, Germany, Italy, Spain and the UK. The later stages also included Portugal. The approach adopted was strongly informed by the UK evaluation and sought to investigate whether the IBM KidSmart initiative had improved the ICT provision offered to pre-school children in settings in France, Germany, Italy, Spain and the UK. The study was again developed as a formative evaluation with a clear objective to in-form future developments of the programme in Europe. This was carried out in a sample of 117 pre-school settings across the five European coun-tries and involved the application of the same instruments as applied in the UK study.

The settings involved in the study were selected as a random, representa-tive (20 per cent) sample of those involved in the KidSmart Early Learn-ing Programme. Comparable *control group* settings were also identified to allow a clear identification of the contribution being made by Kid-Smart. The research partners were trained in the application of each of the instruments, and in the curriculum philosophy and guidance developed by the research directors as part of the DATEC initiative. The European partners were also provided with training resources for application in each country. They translated these resources and contri-buted to early discussions that led to a number of revisions to suit the international contexts. Three two day meetings of the research team took place in the UK over the period of the evaluation to discuss interim results and to ensure inter-rater reliability.

Every setting participating in the evaluation was visited at least three times during twelve months. This intervention period was controlled to allow for international comparisons to be made. We also collaborated closely with the evaluation team in Portugal but the possibilities for com-parison were limited because that study was commissioned some months later than the others.

European evaluation findings

The KidSmart *Early Learning Centres* were found to be highly valued by the early childhood educators, parents and children in all the evaluation countries. Improvements as measured by the use of the ICT ECERS sub-scale were made in five of the six countries evaluated. The progress from 'inadequate' to 'good' ICT practices made by so many of the settings in just one year was outstanding.

	Information handling and communication skills		Access and control of ICT tools		Learning about the uses of ICT	
	Pre-intervention	Final visit	Pre-intervention	Final visit	Pre-intervention	Final visit
UK	2.7	4.9	2.1	5.2	2.3	4.8
Spain	1.0	2.4	1.0	2.8	1.0	2.8
Italy	3.0	5.0	2.7	5.0	1.3	4.4
Germany	1.4	3.9	1.0	4.0	2.4	3.4
France	2.0	4.0	2.3	5.5	1.5	5.3
Portugal	3.1	5.9	3.0	6.0	3.1	5.3

Key 1 = inadequate, 3 = minimal, 4 = fair, 5 = good, 6 = very good, 7 = excellent.

Table 13 The children tended to operate the KidSmart computers in groups of two to five although in Italy a group of four, five or six is not unusual. In Spain, France, Italy, and Portugal most practitioners reported equal use of the units by boys and girls although it may be notable that these countries operate higher adult/child ratios than in the UK and Germany, where most practitioners reported that the boys dominated. Ratios of 1:20 and above were common in Spain (70 per cent) and Italy (63 per cent), with an approximate adult:child ratio of 1:12 typical in the other countries. The ages of the children using the equipment differed significantly between the six countries. While the UK pre-schools catered exclusively for 3 and 4 year olds, our parent survey showed 39 per cent of the French respondents reporting on 5 year old children, and 38 per cent of German parents reporting on 6 year olds. Parents in Portugal, Spain and Italy also reported on significant numbers of 5 and 6 year olds.

How long the *Early Learning Centre* was used in the settings varied a great deal between settings and between countries but there was evidence that practitioners in all six were making increasing use of the equipment. Initially 17 per cent of UK settings reported the equipment being used less than half the available time; by our final visit this was true of only 7 per cent. All the rest reporting that they used it for 90-100 per cent of the time. All of the teachers in France continue to report the *Early Learning Centres* being used for less than 50 per cent of the time. But the number reporting their use for under 30 per cent of the time has dropped from 40 per cent to just 20 per cent. Spain has seen similar improvements, although 59 per cent of settings continue to report the equipment being used for less than half the time available. In 70 per cent of the German settings the equipment is in use for less than 20 per cent of the time and only 10 per cent report use for more than 60 per cent of the time. In Italy the 17% of use initially reported by practitioners has only risen to 20 per cent, although this should be compared with the control group teachers reporting their computers being used for only 5 per cent of the time.

How much of the time practitioners considered the children's use of the *Early Learning Centres* to be educationally productive also increased across the board. In Spain the majority of practitioners initially felt that only 21-60 per cent of the time spent on a computer was productive but they came to consider the children's time at the computer as 100 per cent productive. In the UK 94 per cent of practitioners initially considered 81-100 per cent of the children's time spent on the computer to be productive, in Germany the equivalent percentage was 80 per cent, in Italy 84 per cent, and in France 87 per cent.

Table 14

Percentage of practitioners who felt 81-100 per cent (i.e. most) of the time spent using Early Learning Centres was productive				
	UK	SPAIN	ITALY	GERMANY	FRANCE
First visit	80	0	74	NR	60
Final visit	94	100	84	80	87

The perceptions of educational value did however differ among the countries concerned. The UK had the longest history of ICT curriculum development in early childhood and practitioners followed national guidance that suggested an approach emphasising the value of both 'educational technology' and 'technology education'. In Italy the developments were strongly influenced by concerns to improve access to information and the internet through 'Alphabetization', and a media perspective also dominated in Portugal. In Germany at that time there appeared to be less of a consensus among practitioners. In France and Spain the emphasis was more on the use of the Early Learning Centres as an educational technology to support and reinforce learning across the curriculum.

The Early Childhood practitioners grew increasingly more confident in working with the KidSmart computers in their classrooms:

Table 15

	UK	Spain	Italy	Germany	France	Portugal
The percentage of practitioners who felt very comfortable with the computer						
Visit 1	12	26	10	40	40	18
Final	62	83	74	70	75	70

While many practitioners in the control settings also reported improvements, the improvement in the confidence of the KidSmart practitioners was dramatic. In Portugal the number of practitioners reporting feeling very comfortable increased from 18 per cent to 70 per cent in just six months. This clearly demonstrated the 'user friendliness' of the KidSmart equipment.

The early childhood practitioners involved in the KidSmart programme developed a wider understanding of the nature of ICT. We asked practitioners what they felt children learned from their use of computers and also: 'How is the computer used to assist in the teaching of national or local curriculum requirements (e.g. the UK Early Learning Goals)?' As in the early UK study, we noted a mismatch between practitioner responses to these questions in our pre-intervention phase. It seemed that what the practitioners observed being learned at the computer was quite different from what they intended the children to learn. Our findings showed some evidence of this gap between observations and intentions narrowing to a greater or lesser degree in all the evaluation countries.

Many early years practitioners began with a degree of scepticism about the value of the computers in the pre-school. Their early experiences of the Riverdeep software encouraged a perception of the role of the computer as an educational technology that might be applied in supporting learning, primarily through practice and reinforcement across the curriculum. Early observations of the children's development of hand eye co-ordination and turn taking with the mouse encouraged perceptions of the children's early learning that were dominated by the development of these basic computer and co-operative skills. This notion of the computer as providing 'education technology' also informed many practitioners' conception of 'computer integration' across the curriculum. A deeper understanding of the role of ICT was apparent in Italy, where the emphasis on *Alphabetisation* encouraged a perception of the role of the computer in supporting democratic practices. In the UK and in Portugal an increasing number of practitioners also recognised the part that might be played by the computer as a tool in supporting the development of 'technology education'. For the youngest children, ICT was increasingly being integrated into their socio-dramatic role play and in the most innovative settings children were using the computers creatively for their own productive purposes rather than merely in the application of proprietary curriculum software.

In the final evaluation of the German settings the practitioners reported less potential for curriculum integration. This may have been due to initial over-expectation, or it may be related to the heavier emphasis that was placed on the view of computers as devices 'for learning rather than for playing' (Eirich, 2003). This was reported to be a common practitioner response following the State pressures for improving standards that followed Germany's disappointing performance in the Program for International Student Assessment (PISA) exercise.

As Halverson Pace, an IBM Community Relations and Public Affairs Manager in the USA has argued:

> Although children work well by themselves on the Young Explorers and demonstrate a tremendous capacity to share skills and learn from each other, nothing replaces the active presence of a teacher. (Halverson Pace, 2000)

Aware of the research evidence on this, referred to in previous chapters, we specifically asked the practitioners about how much time adults spent providing children with extension activities or stimulus, providing modelling or demonstration and reinforcing what the child was learning. While a few (8 per cent) UK and German practitioners reported modelling and even less reported some extension work, it is clear that these kinds of ICT-focused support are conspicuously lacking. Of even greater concern is the fact that in every country the percentage of time where adults are working directly with children at the computer was reported to be lower overall than before the intervention. This may be due to the inherent child friendliness of much of the *Riverdeep* software. But this is all especially unfortunate given the research evidence (Sammons *et al*, 2002; 2003). The REPEY research showed that even in the best preschools, adults spend very little time supporting children at the computer and even though qualified teachers are more likely to be present at the computer, adult support is rarely extended beyond two or three minutes (Siraj-Blatchford *et al*, 2003). Yet the *Riverdeep* Early Learning Series software clearly provides many contexts for developing extended activity with adult support, and the *Teachers Guide* offers good resources for curriculum integration.

The digital divide

Another question the evaluation considered was the extent to which the KidSmart Early Learning programme was meeting its stated goals of making a contribution to bridging the digital divide in disadvantaged communities. Our results were encouraging in most countries. For our analysis we adopted the PISA (OECD, 2000) protocol of taking the father's employment as a primary indicator, and where the father was un-employed, absent or of lower status, we took the mother's employment instead. But although there are various international standard classifica-tion systems of occupation, an adequate international index of socio-economic status (SES) had still to be realised. The following tables there-fore show the data collected on the socio-economic status of parents in each country as indicated by the occupational categories defined in the UK standard National Statistics Socio-economic Classification (NS-SEC). This provides a general indication of the parents' socio-economic status and it could be seen that in the case of the UK and Spain the allocations were particularly strongly skewed towards communities who were un-employed or employed in the Technical, Routine and Manual sectors.

Table 16

Percentage of Parents from Lower SES (lower social economic classes)					
	UK	Spain	Italy	Germany	France
Technical, Routine and Manual, Unemployed	75%	77%	40%	47%	38%

Caution is required in interpreting this data; to judge its significance fully, standardised baseline data for the occupational structure of each country is required and this is currently unavailable. It may be that the UK occupational definitions are misleading in these contexts, and in any event it is clear that there were wide variations in the reporting of occu-pational status by parents. In Italy in particular, 51 per cent of the sample classified themselves as 'intermediate' on the NS-SEC five point scale. However, in Germany 25 per cent of the parents, and in Italy 15 per cent, reported themselves members of the 'Managerial and Professional' cate-gory and this may suggest some misunderstanding. The appropriateness of the KidSmart placements in France have also been questioned as it seems that most *Ecole maternelle* settings were already equipped with computers before entering into the KidSmart partnership. Thus they have been better resourced than most other French pre-schools serving disadvantaged, particularly rural communities.

The UK has appropriate national baseline data. This shows that parents employed in the lower supervisory and technical, and semi-routine and routine are significantly over-represented, so the UK KidSmart is un-doubtedly meeting the needs of those most disadvantaged.

Table 17

	Influence Population	General Population
Comparing percentages of population with access to KidSmart and UK population in three Occupational Classes		
Managerial and Professional	12	43
Intermediate	9	19
Routine and Manual	58	38

The digital divide is about more than just access, and as our data in Chapter 4 showed, children in lower socio-economic groups are more likely to be only playing games on their home computer. The children of middle class parents are more likely to be using educational software. This suggests that pre-schools need to work with parents in developing educational practices in the home.

Conclusions

Interestingly, many of the improvements in practice we have reported were not directly related to the specific introduction of the *Early Learning Centres*. It was clear that the KidSmart initiative had supported curriculum development across the full range of ICT curriculum provision. The progress being made in the Spanish pre-schools was especially impressive. The starting point for many of the Spanish pre-schools was very low and in many classes the introduction of the *Early Learning Centres* provided the first curriculum area defined specifically for group work. This had an important impact on many of the teachers and some significant changes were noted in their attitudes towards exploratory free play in the early years. The message that ICT includes more than desktop computers has really caught the imagination of early years teachers in the UK. KidSmart has played a significant part in this by acting as a catalyst for curriculum development and innovation.

There were some signs that the French early childhood practitioners' understandings of ICT education were becoming more sophisticated. While fewer of the control group teachers felt that ICT education in-volved learning about radio and television, more came to understand that it included learning about electronic games and toys, and mobile telephones. All the Italian teachers agreed that ICT could be positively integrated with other activities, especially socio-dramatic play, and a more inclusive understanding of the term Information and Communications Technology (ICT) seems to be developing. Ninety per cent of the German respondents were positive about integration, and 60 per cent reported that this could be extended to socio-dramatic play. In Portugal the teachers' perceptions of the learning potential of the computer changed significantly during the intervention period. They showed a greater awareness of the potential of computers to support learning, identifying many more learning areas than they did at the beginning. Nearly all the Spanish teachers also believed that ICT could be integrated across the curriculum. They considered that this was best achieved by using the computer as a play area in the class. The teachers also increased the number of categories referred to in their definition of ICT. We were interested to observe that when teachers first tried to use the computer as part of the curriculum they realised that children knew more than they expected, and not just about ICT: 'they knew all their colours, or sizes, or numbers'.

The robustness of the KidSmart Young Explorer™ unit, its ease of use and the provision of a suite of programmes accessible directly from the hard drive has had a positive effect. It is said that imitation is the sincerest form of flattery, and a Bejing nursery has copied the design (Image 40). In our opinion one of the strongest features of the design has been the

Image 40

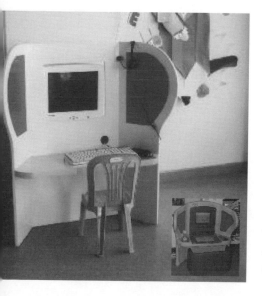

bench seat that encourages children to collaborate, but the retention of the central speaker grill is also valuable. With the speaker fitted behind this grill as originally intended, the wings on each side of the Young Explorer™ somewhat contain the sounds that may distract other children.

As Valerie Halverson Pace (2000) argued, from the very start of KidSmart, the independent evaluations provided by Bank Street College showed that teacher training was critical to success. Yet throughout our European evaluation we found that adequate and appropriate ongoing training was only provided in the German and Portuguese settings. Early Years practitioners continue to call for more training and have said that they now require more curriculum support in integrating their provision for ICT, in the development of practical strategies, and with applying particular exemplary procedures.

Glossary of Technical Terms

Applications: We refer to 'applications of ICT' and distinguish these from ICT (hardware or software) products or 'tools'. While ICT products and tools are mostly created by the ICT industry, 'applications' are always created by teachers and children.

Attachment: Text, sound or image file, which is attached to an e-mail message. When it reaches the addressee, the associated file may be opened or copied to the computer.

Bandwidth: A measure of data (information) transmission. The broader the bandwidth, the quicker the information can be transmitted. Usually measured in kilobits per second (Kbps) or megabits per second (Mbps).

Bits: Binary digits that can have a value of one or zero and can be switched 'on' or 'off'. The basis of all the computer's memory, communication and information storage functions.

Bits per second (Bps): The speed at which the computer can communicate (via its modem) with another computer is normally measured in thousands or millions of bits per second (Kbps: Mbps). See 'Dial-up' and 'Broadband'.

Bluetooth: short-range wireless communications technology developed to enable data connections between a wide range of electronic devices including desktop computers, mobile telephones, personal organisers and their peripheral devices.

Broadband: A class of transmission system which allows large amounts of data (information) to be transferred at high speed. Any internet connection that is faster than 128Kbps has been considered 'broadband'. A typical home cable modem service now provides up to 3Mbps. University and industrial users have access to as much as 2.4 gigabits per second.

Browser: Programme that allows us to search the World Wide Web (e.g. Internet Explorer/Netscape/Mozilla).

Bytes: A byte is 8 binary bits of data. They are usually referred to in specifying the storage space for thousands of bytes (KiloBytes: Kbs), millions of bytes (MegaBytes: Mbs) or billions of bytes (GigaBytes – Gbs). See KiloBytes and GigaBytes.

Cable modem: A means of connecting to the internet using a cable TV network rather than a conventional telephone line.

Cache: A high speed memory unit that operates between the processor and the main memory. A cache can greatly improve the performance of a system but the greater the main memory bandwidth provided the less need there is for cache, so both these influence (along with processor speed) overall computer performance.

Central processing unit (CPU): A microprocessor located on the computer's motherboard that controls the main operations of the computer (see Processor speed below).

Dial-Up: internet access via a telephone line. Dial-up speeds are limited to a maximum of 56Kbps. The service is slow compared to broadband but a lot cheaper.

Digital Subscriber Line (DSL): A broadband service via a telephone line. The service is always on (there is no dial-up) and users can use the internet and the telephone at the same time. There are different varieties of DSL currently offering speeds of up to 8Mbps.

Digital Video Discs (DVDs): Store between 4.7 and 17 GBs (enough to store a one hour movie with a soundtrack and interviews etc).

Domain Name: The first step in obtaining a unique web address or domain name is to contact a company who will check availability and register it for you (normally for two years with the right to renew). This can be done on the internet in just a few minutes. (See e.g. http://www.just-the-name.co.uk)

Download: Copy text, sound or image files from one place on the internet onto your computer.

E-mail: Electronic mail. E-mail provides a set of protocols and programs that allow for the transmission of messages (they may contain any sort of digital file) between users connected to a computer network. E-mail provides asynchronous communication.

Firewall: An internet gateway that limits access e.g. protecting the user from viruses and pornography. Internet Filters are available to protect children, but for more effective protection see BrowserLock (http:\\www.browserlock.com).

GigaBytes (GBs): Billions of bytes. A term normally used to specify the size of hard drives and DVDs.

Graphics Tablet: Provides a digital pencil or stylus for computer drawing or tracing.

Hacker: A term popularly misapplied since the 1960s. Many of the world's best and most enthusiastic programmers consider themselves to be hackers, and they apply the alternative term 'cracker' to refer to those sad individuals who have nothing better to do than use their skills to gain unauthorized entry to other peoples computers, and computer networks, also see virus.

Hard Drive: The storage device inside your computer that holds all the information/data.

Homepage: The first (main) page of a website. To create your own homepage you will first need to select and register a domain name (see above). Most Internet Service Providers provide free web space and even MS Word now provides the facility to take any document and Save As a 'single file web page'. ISPs provide a range of different facilities for uploading and editing web pages. NTL, for example, recommend the use of (and provide a download link for) Terrapin FTP client software.

Hypertext: Texts with marked words that, when clicked upon, forward the user to other places or pages on the internet.

Hypertext mark-up language (Html): The programming language used to create pages on a website.

Import: The process of bringing audio, digital video or fixed images into a software product.

Internet: A worldwide association of interconnected networks of connected computers. This network provides for the transfer of files, remote login, electronic mail, news, search and other services.

Input devices: These are the devices that are used to input information and/or control the programme e.g. keyboards, the mouse, track balls, touch screens etc.

Internet Filtering: Software that gives you the ability to control content displayed, block websites and set up passwords to protect children/adults from pornography, chat sites etc. Popular products include 'ContentProtect' 'Net-Nanny and 'CyberSitter'. See also 'Firewall'.

Integrated services digital network (ISDN): A digital telephone connection providing high speed data transfer (128Kbs).

ISP (Internet Service Provider): Company that supplies internet services to its customers.

ISP Account: An ISP account provides a username and password which allow us to login and access the internet network or a specific service on the internet, such as an email box.

JPG (or jpeg): Format for compressing images, suitable for photographs and for detailed drawings. Even though this is the ideal format for storing and communication photographs on the internet, it may produce images of lower quality than the original.

Kilobytes: Thousands of bytes. The old $5\frac{1}{4}$ 'floppy discs typically stored 360Kbs, and for a long time the maximum storage of a $3\frac{1}{2}$' floppy disc was 800Kbs (now typically 1.4Mbs).

LAN (Local Area Network): a small scale local computer network connected together via cables or Wi-Fi. The network may share a server and/or a single internet access point.

MegaBytes (MBs): A floppy disc stores 1.4 MBs, and that will take the text of an average novel, or about a one minute of video. CD-ROMs store 700 MBs. See also Bytes, Kilobytes and GigaBytes.

Modem: A device used to access the internet via an ISP. It converts digital data into an audio signal to transmit them via telephone lines. In the same way, it reconverts these signals into data. A modem also dials the line, takes the call and controls the transmission speed. See also 'Cable modem', Dial-up, and DSL.

Mouse: A pointing device that provides an arrow on the monitor screen, and allows you to click or drag items across the computer 'desktop'.

Multimedia: A term used to describe content involving pictures, sound and video.

Operating System (OS): The main software program that runs the computer. The most common operating systems are now Windows (95, 98, 2000, XP), Mac OS (8, 9, 10, X), LINUX and UNIX.

Peripheral Device: any external device linked to a computer or micro-processor e.g. a printer, mouse, disk drive, scanner, hands-free headset etc

Processor (or clock) speed: Modern PCs run at clock speeds of 1.6GHz to 3.06GHz or more. At one time this was considered the major factor that determined system performance. Now other factors such as cache size, memory bandwidth, and the Instructions Per Clock (IPC) cycle are considered equally significant.

Random Access Memory (RAM): This provides the computer with temporary storage space it needs to run programmes. Everything in the RAM is lost when you switch your machine off. 256MBs is now generally considered a minimum specification.

Server: These are computers that are set up to 'serve' web pages on the internet.

Scanner: A device for capturing a digital image of a drawing or picture.

Software: Computer programmes (often contrasted with 'hardware' – the physical equipment of a computer system and/or 'liveware' – the human user/operators of computer systems who are sometimes considered to merely complement the hardware and software!).

Universal Resource Locator (URL): The 'address' of a website. They usually (but not always) begin with: http://www.

Virus: A software programme, usually downloaded from the internet, that infiltrates a PC, making something happen that you would rather not (e.g. loss of data).

Web or World Wide Web (WWW): Another name for the internet.

WebCam: A small video camera that usually plugs into the USB socket of your PC. While designed primarily for use on the internet, webcams provide an inexpensive and versatile means of recording and playing back video for a variety of purposes.

Website: Pages posted on the internet. These pages are accessed using a URL and may be maintained by an ISP or other individual or institution with the appropriate server.

Webmail: Electronic mail server, which can be accessed through a Browser.

Wi-Fi (Wireless Fidelity): a high-frequency wireless local area network (W-LAN) based on the IEEE 802.11b standard. It is currently the most common means of wireless networking and operates at 2.4 GHz.

Appendix A: Portfolio Entries

by A b b y

8th Nov '04.

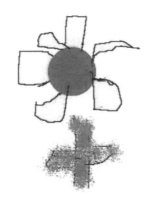

Abby was able to use
the large circle-for the
centre of the flower. She
then drew and filled the
petals. She realised that
she had not filled all the
gaps when the whole screen
turned yellow. Now she
knows to make sure their
are no gaps. Used the
undo button.   PH.

May '05

Katie was able to
change the size of
the brush to create
the features on
'Baby Bears' face and
body.   :) PH.

Appendix B:

DATEC ICT Application Review

Application:
Title (included in):
Publisher:
Supplier:
Age group suitability:

1. The main learning objectives that the application addresses
2. Comparison with other established and alternative approaches to achieving the specified learning objectives
3. Potential for integration with other activities (e.g. topic/ socio-dramatic play)
4. Potential for collaboration/sustained dialogue
5. Implications for classroom or play space layout/organisation
6. Are there underlying values that it reflects?
7. Any comments related to special educational needs
8. Children's evaluation
9. Strongest features
10. Summary

System/hardware requirements: *BBC/Acorn/Mac/Win3.1/ Win95/Win98/2000*

Ease of loading/setting up:	*Difficult*	*Average*	*Easy*
Response (to child's action):	***Fast***	***Average***	***Slow***
Can text be spoken?	*Yes*	*No*	
Child's control over the activity:	*High*	*Low*	
Quality of sound/images:	*Good*	*Poor*	
Can you print-out:	*Yes*	*No*	
Adult support required:	*Short Intro.*	*Long intro.*	
	Continuous	*None*	
Problem solving (if applic.):	*Closed*	*Open*	
Menu accessibility (to children) (/10):	____		
Adult expertise reqd. (/10):	____	**Circle as necessary**	

Appendix C:
ECERS ICT subscale

Item 1 Information handling and Communication Skills

1.1 No or little use is made of ICT in the setting.[1]	3.1 ICT is applied by staff to enhance the print and number environment throughout the setting (e.g. printouts used in emergent literacy/numeracy/labels)	5.1 Staff use the computer during story telling and/or other group activities (e.g. multimedia, talking books, programmable toys, encyclopaedia)	7.1 Children are encouraged to use ICT to share their ideas and discoveries with peers (e.g. displaying their painting in a display or the centre's web page)
1.2 Children are not encouraged to operate the ICT themselves e.g. any available computer, video, television, cassette, telephone etc.[2]	3.2 Children are encouraged to use only the supplied and pre-installed software on the computer (e.g. drill and practice literacy and numeracy programmes)	5.2 Children are encouraged to choose their own applications during free play	7.2 The children are encouraged to provide initial instruction and to help each other to use new programmes and applications
		5.3. The programmes available include open-ended problem solving, adventure games and draw/paint software.[3]	7.3 Children are encouraged to use generic software[4] and other applications for their own purposes e.g. using a paint programme to make a birthday card for a parent
		5.4 In applying the ICT the children make their own choices to produce different outcomes	

1 Computers and programmable toys are not available, mostly ignored or inoperative
2 e.g. switching equipment on and off
3 Applications supporting/demanding creativity
4 Generic software is software designed for a multiplicity of uses, e.g wordprocessing, graphics, database

Item 2 Access and control of ICT tools

1	3	5	7
1.1 Very little pretend or real technology is available for the children's use in the setting[5]	3.1 Children occasionally select and load their own computer programmes under adult supervision	5.1 Children routinely select and load their own computer software	7.1 Children are encouraged and supported in information retrieval e.g. in accessing a CD-Rom encyclopaedia)6 to help them answer a question
1.2 Children are seldom or never given the opportunity to operate ICT e.g. TV, cassette, video, computers etc	3.2 Children have the opportunity to play with computer programmes and/or programmable toys (e.g. Pixie)	5.2 Children are encouraged to operate ICTs and to appreciate that signals and instructions are required to control them	7.2 Children are encouraged in their play to control a wide range of real and/or pretend technologies e.g. alarms, washing machines, video recorders etc
	3.3 Children have access to, and operate for themselves, cassette recorders, video, computers	5.3 Computer software is employed to support learning in a range of subject areas e.g. music and science as well as literacy and numeracy	7.3 Computer software is available to support learning in all subject areas across the curriculum

5 i.e. restricted to telephones, cash registers etc – no programmable toy and no real or pretend computer
6 Or other CD-Rom or internet (non-fiction) information source

Item 3 Learning about the uses of ICT

1	3	5	7
1.1 No references are made to the ICT in the children's homes, the early childhood setting or local environment	3.1 Staff sometimes draw children's attention to the ICT in the setting and in their homes7	5.1 Children's attention is specifically drawn to the ICT in their local environment e.g. through reading stories about technology, visits to supermarket checkouts etc	7.1 Children are encouraged to provide narrative accounts8 of their own and others interactions with ICT e.g. of scanning products through a supermarket checkout, using a cash point, ICT at home
1.2 Children never see the staff using ICT for their own purposes	3.2 Children sometimes see staff using ICT e.g. a school secretary using a word processor	5.2 Children routinely see staff using ICT in pursuit of the educational aims of the setting e.g. searching for information on the www, programming a video recorder, making labels for display, using a mobile telephone	7.2 Staff provide instruction in new applications as a direct response to a child or group of children's interests or expressed needs
	3.3 Pretend or real ICT resources are provided for the children to use in socio-dramatic play environments e.g. home corner	5.3 Play with pretend or real ICT is encouraged and often included in socio-dramatic play	7.3 ICT is integrated into a range of socio-dramatic play environments e.g. in a 'shop' or an 'office' play environment

7 If not directly observed, this item must be included in the settings curriculum scheme or statement

8 e.g. telling each other about their own or others' use of ICT in 'sharing time'

References

6, P. and Jupp, B. (2001) Divided by Information? The 'digital divide'and the implications of the new meritocracy, *Demos*, March http://www.demos.co.uk/catalogue/dividedinformation/

Ager, R. and Kendall, M. Getting it right from the start: a case study of the development of a foundation stage learning and teaching ICT strategy in Northamptonshire, UK, in Wright, J., DcDougall, A, Murnane, J. and Lowe, J. (2003) Young Children and Technologies: International Federation for Information Processing Working Group 3.5, Open Conference, Australian Computer Society, Sydney NSW

Agalianos, A.(Ed.) (2003) European Union-supported educational research 1995-2003: Briefing Papers for Policy Makers, European Commission EUR 20791, http://www.ntua.gr/dep/old/International/LLL/report_education_03.pdf

Alexander, R. (2000) *Culture and Pedagogy: International Comparisons in Primary Education*, Oxford, Blackwell

Alexander, R. (2004) *Towards Dialogic Teaching: Rethinking classroom talk*, York, Dialogos

American Association of University Women Educational Foundation (1998); 'Gender Gaps: Where Schools Still Fail Our Children' http://www.aauw.org/2000/ggpr.html

Anderson, C. and Dill, C. (2000) Video Games and Aggressive Thoughts, *Journal of Personality and Social Psychology*, 78, pp. 772-790.

Antoniety A.(1991). *Why does mental visualization facilitate problem-solving? Advances in Psychology series*, Holland, Elsevier

Bandura, (1986) *Social Foundations of Thought and Action: A Social Cognitive Theory*, Englewood Cliffs, New Jersey, Prentice Hall

Baudrillard, J. (1994) *Simulacra and Simulation.* Ann Arbor, University of Michigan Press

Beauchamp, G. (2004) Teacher use of the Interactive Whiteborad (IWB) in Primary Schools – towards an effective transition framework, *Technology, Pedagogy and Education*, 13, 329-349

Beeching, R (2002) The Insensitive Mouse, http://www.sierratel.com/robprod/insesnsitivemouse.htm

Behar, M. and Silberman, S. (2000) Hello, World: Imagine a machine that speaks your language – and translates it for those who don't, A wired special report on the future of translation, *Issue* 8.05, May 2000 http://www.wired.com/wired/archive/8.05/tpintro.html

Berk, L.E. (2001) *Awakening Children's Minds. How parents and teachers can make a difference.* New York, Oxford University Press.

Black, P. and Wiliam, D. (1998) 'Assessment and classroom learning', *Assessment in Education*, 5, 1, pp7-73

Blázquez, F. (1996). La formación Permanente del Profesorado en España, in Domínguez, E. (coord.) y otros. *Política y Educación (El caso de España y Portugal)* Salamanca, Hespérides, 87-110.

Blok, H., Oostdam, R., Otter, M. and Overmaat, M. (2002) Computer-assisted instruction in support of beginning reading instruction: a review, *Review of Educational Research*, Spring, Vol. 72, pp. 101-130

Bowman, B., Donovan, S. and Burns, S. (Eds.) (2001) *Eager to Learn: Educating our Preschoolers*, Committee on Early Childhood Pedagogy, National Academic Press, Washington USA

Bredenkamp, S. and Copple, C. (Eds.) (1997) *Developmentally Appropriate Practice in Early Childhood Programmes* (revised edition), National Association for the Education of Young Children, Washington DC

British Educational Communications and Technology Agency (Becta) (2003) What the Research Says about using ICT in Maths http://www.becta.org.uk/page_documents/research/wtrs_maths.pdf

British Educational Communications and Technology Agency (Becta) (2004) Using web-based resources in the Foundation Stage, Becta, Coventry; http://www.becta.org.uk/corporate/publications/documents/WBR_foundation.pdf

British Educational Communications and Technology Agency (Becta) (2005) Planning to purchase an interactive whiteboard http://www.becta.org.uk/leaders/leaders.cfm?section=3_1&id=3173

Brooker, E. and Siraj-Blatchford, J. (2002) 'Click on Miaow!': How children of three and four experience the nursery computer, *Contemporary Issues in Early Childhood*, Volume 3, Number 2, 2002

Buckingham D and Scanlon, M. (2004) Connecting the family? 'Edutainment' web sites and learning in the home, *Education, Communication and Information*, Vol. 4, No. 2-3., 271.

Burns, C., and Myhill, D. (2004) Interactive or inactive? A consideration of the nature of interaction in whole class teaching, *Cambridge Journal of Education*, 34(1) 35-49

Burts, D., Hart, C., Charlesworth, R. and Kirk, L. (1990) 'A comparison of frequency of stress behaviours observed in kindergarten children in classrooms with developmentally appropriate versus developmentally inappropriate instructional practices', *Early Childhood Research Quarterly*, Vol. 5 pp. 407-423

Carioca, V. (1997) *Validação de uma escala de atitudes de docentes relativamente à utilização da informática educativa na sua formação continua*, Tese de doutoramento, apresentada em Janeiro à Universidade da Extremadura (Espanha).

Carioca, V., Siraj-Blatchford, J., Pramling Samuelsson, I., Sheridan, S., Passarinho, A., and Saúde, S. (2005) ICT in the Early Years: A Handbook for trainers, Kinderet, Escola Superior de Educação, Beja, Portugal http://www.eseb.ipbeja.pt/kinderet/

Carplay, J. and van Oers, B. (1993) Models for learning and the problem of classroom discourse, *Voprosy Psichologii* 4, 20-26

Carr, M. and Claxton, G. (2002). Tracking the development of learning dispositions. *Assessment in Education: Principles, Policy and Practice*, 9 (1)

Carter, V. (2005) Finding the point of it all, http://www.camelsdale.w-sussex.sch.uk/powerpoint_in_yr.asp

Childres, T., and Post, J. (1975). *The information-poor in America*. New Jersey, Scarecrow Press

Christakis, D., Zimmerman, F., DiGiuseppe, D., and McCarty, C. (2004) Early Television Exposure and Subsequent Attentional Problems in Children, *Pediatrics* Vol. 113 No. 4 April 2004, pp. 708-713

Clark, P., Griffing, P. and Johnson, L. (1989). Symbolic play and ideational fluency as aspects of the evolving divergent cognitive style in young children. *Early Child Development and Care*, 51, 77 88

Clements, D. (1994) The uniqueness of the computer as a learning tool: Insights from research and practice. In Wright J., and Shade, D. (Eds.), *Young children: Active learners in a technological age*. Washington, DC, NAEYC

Clements, D. (2002) From exercises and tasks to problems and projects – unique contributions of computers to innovative mathematics education, *The Journal of Mathematical Behaviour*, 19, (1), pp. 9-47

Clements, D. and Gullo, D. (1984) Effects of computer programming on young children's cognition, *Journal of Educational Psychology*, 76, pp1051-8

Coe, R. (2002) It's the Effect Size, Stupid: What effect size is and why it is important, Paper presented at the Annual Conference of the British Educational Research Association, University of Exeter, 12-14 September 2002, Online 11th March 2005 at: http://www.leeds.ac.uk/educol/documents/00002182.htm

Comstock, G. (1991) *Television and the American Child*. Orlando, Academic Press

Cooper, B., and Brna, P. (2004) A Classroom of the Future, in Siraj-Blatchford, J. (Ed.) *Developing New Technologies for Young Children*, Stoke on Trent, Trentham Books

Cordes, C. and Miller, E. (Eds.) (2000) Fool's gold: A critical look at computers in childhood. College Park, MD, USA: Alliance for Childhood, Online 11th march

2005 at: http://www.allianceforchildhood.org/projects/computers/computers_reports.htm

Cox, M., Webb, M., Abbott, C., Blakeley, B., Beauchamp, T. and Rhodes, V. (2003) *ICT and pedagogy: A review of the research literature, ICT in Schools* Research and Evaluation Series No.18 Produced by Becta for the Department for Education and Skills, DfES Publications

Crook C. (1994) *Computers and the Collaborative Experience of Learning*, London, Routledge

Crook, C. (2003) cited in International Business Machines (IBM) (2003) Early Learning in the Knowledge Society: Report on a European Conference, 22-23rd May, Brussels

Department for Education and Skills (DfES) (2001) *Key Stage 3 National Strategy: framework for teaching mathematics*, London DfES

Department for Education and Skills (DfES) (2003) Survey of Information and Communications Technology in Schools 2003, Online 11th March 2005 at: http://www.dfes.gov.uk/rsgateway/DB/SBU/b000421/index.shtml

Department for Education and Skills (DfES) (2003) *Towards a unified e-learning strategy*, Department for Education and Skills, consultation document, 2003, at dfes.gov.uk

Department of Trade and Industry (DTI) (2000) *Closing the digital divide: information and communication technologies in deprived areas*: a report by Policy Action Team 15 London, DTI.

DeVries, R. (1997) Piaget's Social Theory, *Educational Researcher*, Vol. 26 No. 2 March

Dois, W. and Mugny, G. (1984) *The Social Development of the Intellect*, Oxford, Pergamon Press

Donaldson (1978) *Children's Minds*. London, Fontana

Dowling, M. (2005) *Supporting Young Children's Sustained Shared Thinking: An Exploration of Training Materials*, Early Education

Dunn, J., Brown, J., Slomkowski, C., Tesla, C. and Youngblade, L. (1991) 'Young children's understandings of other children's feelings and beliefs: Individual differences and their antecedents.' *Child Development* 62, 1352-1366.

Dweck, C. (2000) *Self theories: Their role in motivation, personality and development*, Philadelphia, Taylor and Francis

Education Development Centre Inc., Centre for Children and Technology, International Page, EDC/CCT – KidSmart 2000 – International Page ibm.com/ibm/ibmgives/edc/index.htm

Edwards, C, and Springate. K. (1995) The Lion Comes Out of the Stone: helping young children achieve their creative potential. *Dimensions of Early Childhood* 23(4, Fall), 24-29.

Edwards, C. and Hiler, C. (1993) *A Teacher's Guide To The Exhibit: 'The Hundred Languages Of Children'*, College of Human Environmental Sciences, University of Kentucky, Lexington, Kentucky

Eirich, H. (2003) Unpublished correspondence associated with J. and I. Siraj-Blatchford (2004a)

Epstein, J. (1996) Perspective and Previews on Research and Policy for School, Family and Community Partnerships, in Booth, A. and Dunn, J. (Eds) *Family-School Links: How do they affect educational outcomes?* Mahwah, NJ, Lawrence Erlbaum

European Commission (2001) Knowledge Society, Employment, Social Affairs and Equal Opportunities. http://europa.eu.int/comm/employment_social/knowledge_society/index_en.htm

Facer, K (2002) 'What do we mean by the digital divide?' paper presented at invited symposium on the Digital Divide, Coventry, February 19th, 2002 http://www.interactiveeducation.ac.uk/outcomes.htm

Facer, K., Furlong, J., Sutherland, R. and Furlong, R. (2000) Home is where the hardware is: young people, the domestic environment and 'access' to new technologies, in Hutchby, I., and Moran-Ellis, J. (Eds.) *Children, Technology and Culture*, London, Falmer

Fatouros, C. (1995). Young children using computers: Planning appropriate learning experiences. *Australian Journal of Early Childhood*, 20, 2, pp. 1-6.

Finch, S. and Kitchen, S. (2004) Evaluation of Curriculum Online: Report of the baseline survey of Foundation Stage providers, National Centre for Social Research, Prepared for Department for Education and Skills, Online 11th March 2005 at: http://www.becta.org.uk/page_documents/research/curriculum_online/foundation_stage_report.pdf

Fine, C. and Thornbury, M. (1998) Control and literacy, *Micros and Primary Education* (MAPE) Special focus on Literacy, Autumn

Fletcher-Flinn, C. and Suddendorf, T. (1996) Do computers affect the mind? *Journal of Educational Computing Research*, 15 (2) pp.97-112

Forman, E. (1984) The role of peer interaction in the social construction of mathematical knowledge, *International Journal of Educational Research*, 13, pp. 55-69

Galton, M. (2000) Integrating Theory and Practice: Teachers' Perspectives on Educational Research, TLRP Annual Conference, 2000. Online 11th March 2005 at: http://www.tlrp.org/acadpub/Galton2000.pdf

Galton, M., Hargreaves, L., Comber, C., Wall, D. and Pell, A. (1999) *Inside the Primary Classroom: 20 Years On*, London, Routledge

Giacquinta, B.J., Baucer, A.J. and Levin, J. (1993) *Beyond technology's promise.* Cambridge, Cambridge University Press.

Glasner, J. (2002) Of PowerPoint and Pointlessness, Wired News, http://wired-vig.wired.com/news/school/0,1383,54675,00.html

Greeno, J.G. (1991) Number sense as situated knowing in a conceptual domain. *Journal in Research in Mathematics Education*, 22, 170-218.

Hall, N. (1987) *The emergence of literacy*. Portsmouth, NH, Heinemann Educational Books

Halverson Pace, V. (2000) Lessons in Funding Technology: IBM's Global KidSmart Early Learning Program, Giving Forum Online, Winter, http://www.mcf.org/mcf/forum/ibm.htm

Hancox, R., Milne, B., Poulton, R. (2005) Association of Television Viewing During Childhood With Poor Educational Achievement, Arch Pediatr Adolesc Med. 2005; 159: 614-618.

Hannon, P. and James, A. (1990) Parents' and Staff' Perspectives on Pre-school Literacy Development', *British Educational Research Journal*, 16, 3

Hargreaves, L., Moyles, J., Merry, R., Paterson, F., Pell, A., Esarte-Sarries, V. (2003) How do primary school teachers define and implement 'interactive teaching' in the National Literacy Strategy in England, *Research Papers in Education* 18(3), 217-236

Hargreaves, D. (2005) About Learning: Report of the Learning Working Group, Demos http://www.demos.co.uk/catalogue/aboutlearning

Harms, T., Clifford, R.M., and Cryer, D. (1998) *Early Childhood Environment Rating Scale, Revised Edition* (ECERS-R), Columbia, Teachers College Press.

Haugland, S. (2000) Early Childhood Classrooms in the 21st Century: Using Computers to Maximise Learning. *Young Children*, 55, 1, pp. 12-18.

Healey, J. (1998) *Failure to Connect*, New York, Simon and Shuster

Hewison, J. (1988) 'The long term effectiveness of parental involvement in reading: a follow-up study to the Haringey reading project', *British Journal of Educational Psychology*, 58, pp.184-190.

Higgins, C. (1995) Information Technology in Ashcroft, K., Palacio, D., *The Primary Teacher's Guide to the New National Curriculum*, Routledge

Hohmann, M. and Weikart, D.P. (1995) *Educating Young Children*. Michigan:,High/Scope Educational Research Foundation.

Howes, C. and Matheson, C.C. (1992) Sequences in the Development of Competent Play with Peers: social and pretend play, *Developmental Psychology*, 28, pp. 961-974

Hoyles, C. (1985) What is the Point of group discussion in mathematics? *Studies in Mathematics*, Vol. 16 pp205-24

Humphries, P. (2005) Peter Humphreys replies, BECTA ICT advice for teachers: Ask an Expert http://www.ictadvice.org.uk/index.php?section=ae&page=question&theme=77&qid=2261&pagenum=6&NextStart=4

Huxley A (1958) *Propaganda in a Democratic Society in Brave New World Revisited*, London/New York, Chatto and Windus/Harper & Collins. http://ics.leeds.ac.uk/papers/pmt/exhibits/1053/huxley.pdf

International Business Machines (IBM) (2003) Early Learning in the Knowledge Society: Report on a European Conference, 22-23rd May, Brussels

Ioannidou I. and Dimitracopoulou A. (2004). Young Children Collaborating to use Maps during Technology based Distributed Learning Activities. In *Proceedings of 6th International Conference of Mathematics Teaching*, October 2003, Volos, Greece.

James, M., Pollard, A. Rees, G., Taylor, C. (2003) *Of Warrants and Warranting: building confidence in our conclusions*, TLRP Occasional Paper.

Jessen, C. and Holm-Sorensen, B. (2000) It Isn't Real: children, computer games, violence and reality, in C. Von Feilitzen and U. Carlsson (Eds) *Children and Media Violence: Yearbook 2000, Children in the New Media Landscape*, pp. 119-122. Göteborg

Judge, P. (2000) A Lesson in Computer Literacy from India's Poorest Kids Business Week Online, March 2, http://www.businessweek.com/bwdaily/dnflash/mar2000/nf00302b.htm?scriptFramed

UNESCO International Clearinghouse on Children and Violence on the Screen, NORDICOM, Göteborgs University.

Kane, S. R. (1994) 'Shared meaning in young children's peer relationships: The development of practical social-cognitive know-how. Paper presented at the 24th Annual Symposium of the Jean Piaget Society

Kenner, C., Arju, T., Gregory, E., Jessel, J., and Ruby, M. (20040 Report on a research project with children and grandparents in East London, *Primary Practice: The Journal of the National Primary Trust*, No. 38, Autumn

Kennington, L. (2005) Video: Gamesley Early Excellence Centre, available online at; http://www.gamesleyeec.org.uk/ict.asp

Larkin, S. (2000) How can we discern metacognition in year one children from interactions between students and teacher, Paper presented at ESRC Teaching and Learning Research Programme Conference, 9th November

Leontiev, A. (1981) *Problems of the Development of Mind*, Moscow University Press, Moscow

Lewin, C. (2000). Exploring the effects of talking books software in UK primary classrooms. *Journal of Research in Reading*, 23, 2, pp. 149-157.

Lewis, C., Freeman, N.H., Kyriadicou, C., Maridaki-Kassotaki, K. and Berridge, D. (1996) Social Influences on False Belief Access: specific sibling influences or general apprenticeship? *Child Development*, 67, pp. 2930-2947

Light, P. and Butterworth, G. (Eds.) (1992) *Context and cognition: ways of learning and knowing*, Hemel Hempstead, Harvester Wheatsheaf

Linderoth, J. and Lantz-Andersson, A. (2002) Electronic exaggerations and virtual worries: Mapping research of computer games relevant to the understanding of children's game play, *Contemporary Issues in Early Childhood* Volume 3 Number 2, Available online at http://www.triangle.co.uk/ciec/content/pdfs/3/issue3_2.asp

Loveless, A. (2002) *Literature Review in Creativity, New Technologies and Learning,* Report 4, NESTA Futurelab Series

Luckin, R.; Connolly, D.; Plowman, L. and Airey, S. (2003) *Out of the Box, but in the Zone? Can digital toy technology provide a more able peer for young learners?,* Proceedings of the International Conference on Artificial Intelligence in Education 2003

Luckin, R., D. Connolly, L. Plowman and S. Airey (2003). With a little help from my friends: children's interactions with interactive toy technology. *Journal of Computer Assisted Learning, special issue on Children and Technology.* 19 (2) 165-176.

Marcon, R. (2002). Moving up the grades: Relationship between preschool model and later school success. *Early Childhood Research and Practice,* 4 (1).

Matthew, K. (1997). A Comparison of the Influence of Interactive CDROM Storybooks and Traditional Print Storybooks on Reading Comprehension. *Journal of Research on Computing in Education,* 29,3, pp. 263-275.

McKenzie, W. (1994) The Video Game as Emergent Media Form, *Media Information,* Australia, 71, pp. 21-30.

McNulty, M. (2003) Social Justice and the Internet, Paper Presented to the 'Revisioning Boundaries' Conference, Wilfrid Laurier University, April 2003. http://www.arts.uwaterloo.ca/~mjmcnult/social_justice_overhead.htm

McPake, J., Stephen, C., Plowman, L., Sime, D. and Downey, S. (2004) *Already at a Disadvantage? ICT in the Home and Children's Preparation for Primary School,* Coventry, Becta, http://www.ioe.stir.ac.uk/Research/Briefings/becta%20summary.pdf

Mirandanet (2005) Interactive Whiteboards: new tools, new pedagogies, new learning?, Case Studies on http://www.mirandanet.dial.pipex.com/ftp/whiteboard.pdf

Mitra, S (2001) Cited in; Delhi children make play of the net, BBC World Service's Go Digital, 27 August, 2001, http://news.bbc.co.uk/1/hi/sci/tech/1502820.stm

Mroz, M., Smith, F. and Hardman, F. (2000) The Discourse of the Literacy Hour, *Cambridge Journal of Education,* 30(3) 379-390

Nager, N. (1999) Evaluation of Use of IBM Kidsmart Program, unpublished report, New York, Bank Street College

Nager, N. (2000) Evaluation of use of IBM Kidsmart Program: Progress towards desirable outcomes, unpublished report, New York, Bank Street College,

National Association for the Education of Young Children (NAEYC) (1998) Position Statement: Technology and Young Children – ages 3 through 8, Online 11th March 2005: http://www.naeyc.org/about/positions/pdf/PSTECH98.PDF

National Centre for Health Statistics (2000) 2000 CDC Growth Charts: United States http://www.cdc.gov/growthcharts/

National Grid for Learning (NGfL) Scotland (2002) ICT in Pre-school Consultation Paper http://www.ngflscotland.gov.uk/earlyyears/resources/consult_paper.pdf

National Reading Panel (2000) *Report of the National Reading Panel – Teaching Children to Read: An evidence based assessment of the scientific research literature on reading and its implications for reading instruction,* Washington DC, US Government Printing Office

Nobel, D. (1979) *Forces of Production: A Social History of Industrial Automation,* Alfred A Knopf, New York.

Norvik, P. (2004) PowerPoint: shot with its own bullets, http://www.norvig.com/lancet.html#refs

OECD (2001) Science, Technology and Industry Scoreboard 2001, Towards a knowledge-based economy, http://www1.oecd.org/publications/e-book/92-2001-04-1-2987/.

OECD (2001) Knowledge and Skills for Life: First Results from PISA 2000, OECD, http://oecdpublications.gfi-nb.com/cgi-bin/OECDBookShop.storefront/

Oerter, R. (1993) *The Psychology of Play: An activity oriented approach,* Quintessenz, Munich

Office for Standards in Education (OFSTED) (2000) The quality of nursery education for three and four-year-olds 1999-2000, http://ofsted.gov.uk/publications/docs/767.pdf

Pacey, A. (1983) *The Culture of Technology,* The MIT Press, Cambridge Mass.

Papert, S. (1980) *Mindstorms: Children, Computers and Powerful Ideas,* New York, Basic Books

Papert, S. (2001) Keynote address to the special forum on 'ICT and Education at the OECD on 2nd April, reproduced in full in OECD (2001) .Schooling for tomorrow – learning to change: ICT in schools, Online 11th March 2005 at http://www1.oecd.org/publications/e-book/9601131E.PDF

Pelligrini, A., Galda, L., and Flor, D. (1997). Relationships, Individual Differences and Children's Use of Literate Language, *British Journal of Educational Psychology* 1997 Jun, 67 (Pt 2):139-52

Perner, J., Leekam, S.R. and Wimmer, H. (1994) Three-Year-olds' Difficulty with False Belief, *British Journal of Developmental Psychology,* 5, pp. 125-137

Piaget, J. (1969) *The Mechanisms of Perception,* London, Routledge and Kegan Paul.

PJB Associates (Eds.) (2003) New Perspectives for Learning (Editorial) of *New Perspectives for Learning,* Issue 5, April edition (publication dedicated to reporting on 'Insights from European Union Research on Education and Training') http://www.pjb.co.uk/npl/npl5.pdf

Plowman, L. and Stephen, C. (2003) A 'benign addition'? A review of research on ICT and pre-school children. *Journal of Computer-Assisted Learning.* 19 (2). Also see Ict In Pre-School: A 'Benign Addition?, Learning and Teaching Scotland, Online 11th March 2005 at: http://www.ltscotland.org.uk/earlyyears/files/benignaddition.pdf

Plowman, L. and Luckin, R (2004) Summary Of Research: Exploring And Mapping Interactivity With Digital Toy Technology Esrc Project L328253009 Http://Www.Ioe.Stir.Ac.Uk/Cachet/Docs/Summary_L328253009.Pdf

Pramling, I (1990) *Learning to learn: a study of Swedish pre-school children*. New York: Springer-Verlag

Qualifications and Curriculum Authority (QCA) and Department for Education and Emplyment (DfES) (2000) *Curriculum Guidance for the Foundation Stage*, London, QCA/DfES

Qualifications and Curriculum Authority (QCA) (2004) *Information and communication technology 2003/4 annual report on curriculum and assessment*, October, QCA/04/1470, QCA http://www.qca.org.uk/downloads/11919_ict _annual_report_curric_assess_03_04.pdf

Rathbun, A and West, J. (2003) *Young Children's Access to Computers in the Home and at School in 1999 and 2000*, National Center for Education Statistics, U.S. Department of Education Institute of Education Sciences

Reilly, J., Coyle, J, Kelly, Burke, G, Grant, S, and Paton, J. (2003a) An objective method for measurement of sedentary behavior in 3- to 4-year olds., *Obesity Research*. 11(10):1155-1158. October

Reilly, J. and McDowell, Z. (2003b) Physical activity interventions in the prevention and treatment of paediatric obesity: systematic review and critical appraisal, Symposium on 'Physical activity, energy expenditure and obesity', A joint meeting of the Nutrition Society and the Aberdeen Centre for Energy Regulation and Obesity, University of Aberdeen, Scotland, on 23-24 July 2002, Proceedings of the Nutrition Society (2003), 62, 611-619

Russ, S. (2003) Play and Creativity: developmental Issues, *Scandinavian Journal of Educational Research*, Vol. 47, No. 3, 2003

Russ, S., Robins, A., and Christiano, B. (1999). Pretend play: Longitudinal prediction of creativity and affect in fantasy in children. *Creativity Research Journal*, 12(2), 129-139.

Russell, N., and Stafford, N. (2002) *Trends in ICT Access and Use*, Taylor Nelson Sofres: Social Report No 358, DfES

Rutter, M. (1985). Family and school influences on cognitive development, *Journal of Child Psychology and Psychiatry*, 26, 683-704.

Sakamoto, A. (2000) Video Games and Violence – controversy and research in Japan, in C. Von Feilitzen and U. Carlsson (Eds) *Children and Media Violence: Yearbook 2000, Children in the New Media Landscape*, pp. 61-78. Göteborg: UNESCO International Clearinghouse on Children and Violence on the Screen, NORDICOM, Göteborgs University.

Sammons, P., Sylva, K., Melhuish, M., Siraj-Blatchford, I., Taggart, B. and Elliot, K. (2002), *Technical Paper 8a – Measuring the Impact of Pre-school on Children's Cognitive Progress*. Institute of Education, University of London. London.

Sammons, P., Sylva, K., Melhuish, M., Siraj-Blatchford, I., Taggart, B. and Elliot, K. (2003) *Technical Paper 8b – Measuring the Impact of Pre-school on Children's*

Social/behavioural Development. Institute of Education, University of London. London.

Sanger, J. (1997) *Young Children, Video and Computer Games: Issues for Teachers,* London, Flamer

Schaffer, R. (1996) *Social Development,* Oxford, Blackwell

Schweinhart, L.J. and Weikart, D.P. (1997). 'The High/Scope Preschool Curriculum Comparison through Age 23' in *Early Childhood Research Quarterly,* 12, pp. 117-143.

Selwyn, N. (1997) 'Teaching Information Technology to the 'Computer Shy': a theoretical perspective on a practical problem', *Journal of Vocational Education and Training,* 49/3, pp. 395-408. http://www.triangle.co.uk/vae/49-03/selwyn.pdf

Selwyn, N. (1999) 'Resisting the Technological Imperative: Issues in Researching the 'Effectiveness' of Technology in Education' from the online journal Compute-Ed, Vol 5 Online 11th March 2005 at: http://pandora.nla.gov.au/nph-arch/2000/Z2000-Jun-5/http://computed.coe.wayne.edu/Vol5/Selvyns.html

Siraj-Blatchford, I. (1999) Early Childhood Pedagogy: Practices, Principles and Research in P. Mortimore (Ed) *Understanding Pedagogy and its Impact on Learning,* pp. 20-45 London: Paul Chapman.

Siraj-Blatchford, I. and Siraj-Blatchford, J. (2000) *More than Computers: Information and Communications Technology in the Early Years,* London, Early Education (The British Association for Early Childhood Education)

Siraj-Blatchford, I., Sylva, K., Muttock, S., and Gilden, R. (2002) *Effective Pedagogy in the Early Years,* Research Report 356, DfES, London

Siraj-Blatchford, I., Sylva, K., Taggart, B., Sammons, P. and Melhuish, E. (2003) *The EPPE case studies Technical Paper 10,* University of London, Institute of Education/DfES.

Siraj-Blatchford, J. (2004) *Developing New Technologies for Young Children,* Stoke on Trent, Trentham Books

Siraj-Blatchford, J. and MacLeod-Brudenell, I. (1999) *Supporting Science, Design and Technology in the Early Years,* Buckingham, Open University Press

Siraj-Blatchford, J. and Siraj-Blatchford, I. (2000a) IBM KidSmart Early Learning Programme: UK Evaluation Report – Phase 1 (2000-2001), IBM White Paper, London, IBM http://www.ibm.com/ibm/ibmgives/downloads/kidsmart_eval_sum_English.pdf

Siraj-Blatchford, J. and Siraj-Blatchford, I. (2002b) Developmentally Appropriate Technology in Early Childhood: 'video conferencing', *Contemporary Issues in Early Childhood,* Vol. 3 No. 2 pp 216 -225

Siraj-Blatchford, J. and Siraj-Blatchford, I. (2004a) IBM KidSmart Early Learning Programme European Evaluation Report: France, Germany, Italy, Portugal, Spain and UK, Final report June:- Phase 2 (2001-2003), IBM White Paper

Siraj-Blatchford, J. and Siraj-Blatchford, I. (2004b) Interim Report on the Northamptonshire ICT Strategy Evaluation, unpublished report

Siraj-Blatchford, J. and Whitebread, D. (2003) *Supporting Information and Communications Technology in the Early Years*, Maidenhead, Open University Press

Slomskowski, C. and Dunn, J. (1996) 'Young children's understanding of other people's beliefs and feelings and their connected communication with friends.' *Developmental Psychology*, 32, (3), 442-447.

Smilansky, S. (1968). *The Effects of Sociodramatic Play on Disadvantaged Pre-school Children*. New York: John Wiley and Sons.

Smilansky, S. (1990) Sociodramatic play: Its relevance to behavior and achievement in school. In Klugman, E. and Smilansky, S. (Eds.), *Children's Play and Learning*. New York: Teacher's College.

Smith, F., Hardman, F., Wall, K. and Mroz, M. (2004) Interactive Whole Class Teaching in the National Literacy and Numeracy strategies, *British Educational Research Journal*, 30, 395-411

Stanton, D., O'Malley, C., Bayon, V., Hourcade, J., Sundblad, Y., Fast, C., Cobb, S., Taxen, G., and Benford, S. (2004) The Kidstory Project: developing collaborative storytelling tools for children, with children, in Siraj-Blatchford, J. (Ed.) *Developing New Technologies for Young Children*, Stoke on Trent, Trentham Books

Statt, D.A. (1998) *The concise dictionary of psychology* (3rd ed.). London and New York, Routledge

Steyaert, J. (2002). Inequality and the digital divide: myths and realities. In S. Hick and J. McNutt (Eds.), *Advocacy, activism and the internet* (pp. 199-211). Chicago, Lyceum Press.

Steyaert, J., and Gould, N. (2004) The rise and fall of the digital divide. In J. Graham, M. Jones and S. Hick (Eds.), *Digital Divide and Back: Social Welfare, Technology and the New Economy*, Toronto, University of Toronto.

Strayer, F. et Cazenave-Tapie, P. (2002) *Technologies d'Information et de Communication et Pratiques Pédagogiques en Maternelle*, Laboratoire Dévelopement, Contextes et Cultures Université de Toulouse II – Le Mirail

Sylva, K., Bruner, J. and Genova, P. (1976) *The role of play in the problem solving of children 3-5 years old*. In Bruner, J., Jolly, A., and Sylva, K. (Eds) Play. New York: Basic Books.

Sylva, K. and Nabuco, M. (1996). 'Research on quality in the curriculum', *International Journal of Early Childhood*, 28, 2, 1-6.

Sylva, K., Siraj-Blatchford, I., Taggart, B. Melhuish, E., Sammons, P., (1999) *The Effective Provision of Pre-School Education (EPPE) Project: Technical Paper 6a Characteristics of Pre-School Environments*, University of London/DfEE

Sylva, K., Siraj-Blatchford, I., and Taggart, B. (2003) *Early Childhood Environment Rating Scale – Extension (ECERS-E): Four Curricular Subscales*. Stoke on Trent, Trentham Books

Sylva, K. Melhuish, E., Sammons, P., Siraj-Blatchford, I. and Taggart, B. (2004). *The Effective Provision of Pre-School Education (EPPE) Project: Technical Paper 12 – The final report*. London, DfES / Institute of Education, University of London.

Tamburrini, J. (1982) Play and the role of the teacher. *Early Childhood Development and Care* 8.

Tanner, H., Jones, S., Kennewell, S. and Beauchamp, G. (2005) Interactive Whole Class Teaching and Interactive White Boards, paper presented at Building Connections: Research, theory and practice Conference, Mathematics Education Research Group of Australasia, July 7-9, 2005, Melbourne

Tan-Niam, C.L.S., Wood, D.J. and O'Malley, C. (1998) 'A cross-cultural perspective on children's theories of mind and social interaction.' *Early Child Development and Care*, 144, 55-67.

Tan-Niam, C.L.S., Wood, D.J. and O'Malley, C. (1999) 'Play initiation, reciprocity and theory of mind.' *The Australian Journal of Research in Early Childhood Education*, 6 (2), 73-83.

Tan-Niam, C.L.S., Wood, D.J. and O'Malley, C. (2000) 'Play interactions and understanding other minds: a cross-cultural study.' *The Australian Journal of Research in Early Childhood Education*, 7 (1), 99-112.

Thouvenelle, S., Borunda, M. and McDowell, C. (1994) Replicating inequities: Are we doing it again? In Wright, J. and Shade, D (Eds.) *Young children: Active learners in a technological age*, Washington, DC, NAEYC.

Tizard, B. and Hughes, M. (1988) Learning at Home: Living and talking together in Cohen, A. (Ed) *Early Education: The Parents' Role. A Source book for teachers.*

Turkle, S. (1995) *Life on the Screen: identity in the age of the Internet*, New York, Simon and Schuster.

UNARETE (2002) UNARETE Digital Democracy, Internet, Alfabetization http://www.unarete.org

Vanderberg, B. (1980). Play, problem-solving and creativity. In Rubin, K. (Ed.), *Children's Play: New directions for child development*, San Francisco, Jossey-Bass.

van Leeuwen, L. (2004) How children contribute to design of technology for there own use, in Siraj-Blatchford, J. (Ed.) *Developing New Technologies for Young Children*, Stoke on Trent, Trentham Books

van Oers, B (1999) Teaching Opportunities in Play, in Hedegaard, M and Lompscher, J., *Learning Activity and Development*, Aarhus University Press, Aarhus

Vygotsky, L. (1978) *Mind in Society: The Development of Higher Psychological Processes*, Harvard University Press, Cambridge Mass

Vygotsky, L. (2004) Imagination and creativity in childhood. *Journal of Russian and East European Psychology* 42, 1, 4-84

Wang, C. and Ching, C. (2003) Social Construction of Computer Experience in a First-Grade Classroom: Social Processes and Mediating Artifacts, Paper Presented at AERA 2003 in Symposium: Perspectives on Studying Artifacts in Physical and Virtual Learning Environments. Online 11th March 2005 at: http://lrs.ed.uiuc.edu/aera/03/artifacts/AERA03-Wang.PDF

Warschauer, M. (2003) *Technology and Social Inclusion, rethinking the digital divide.* Cambrigde, MIT press

Wells, G. and Meija-Arauz, R. (2001) Toward Dialogue In The Classroom: Learning and Teaching Through Inquiry, Manuscript in review for Working papers on Culture, Education and Human Development, http://www.uam.es/otros/ptcedh/enrevision/ref05_02.htm

Wimmer, H. and Perner, J. (1983) Beliefs about beliefs: Representation and constraining function of wrong beliefs in young children's understanding of deception. *Cognition*, 13, 103-128.

Wood, D. (1988) *How children think and learn.* Cambridge, MA, Blackwell.

Wood, D. (2003) Think Again: Hindsight, Insight and Foresight on ICT in Schools, European Schoolnet, Online 11th March 2005 at: http://www.eun.org/insight-pdf/ernist/David_Wood_Think_Again.pdf

Wood, E. and Attfield, J. (1997) *Play, Learning and the Early Childhood Curriculum.* London. Paul Chapman Publishing

Yelland, N. (1999) Reconceptualising schooling with technology for the 21st century. *Information Technology in Childhood Education Annual*, pp. 39-59.

Index